Real Education

Real Education

FOUR SIMPLE TRUTHS FOR BRINGING

AMERICA'S SCHOOLS BACK TO REALITY

CHARLES MURRAY

CROWN
FORUM
NEW YORK

Published in the United States by Crown Forum, an imprint of the Crown
Publishing Group, a division of Random House, Inc., New York.

www.crownpublishing.com

Crown Forum and the Crown Forum colophon are trademarks of
Random House, Inc.

Library of Congress Cataloging-in-Publication Data

Murray, Charles A.
Real education : four simple truths for bringing America's schools back
to reality / Charles Murray.—1st ed.
p. cm.
Includes bibliographical references and index.
1. Educational accountability—United States.   2. Education—United
States—1965-   3. Public schools—United States.   I. Title.
LB2806.22.M87 2008
370.973—dc22
2008009178

ISBN 978-0-307-40538-8

Printed in the United States of America

Design by Leonard W. Henderson

10   9   8   7   6   5   4   3   2   1

First Edition

To Chris DeMuth,
another Captain with a mighty heart

Contents

Acknowledgments

eal Education owes its existence to an e-mail from Tunku Varadarajan, then the editor of the *Wall Street Journal's* op-ed page, on December 28, 2006, asking if I had anything I wanted to say in print. I did. I wanted to bash No Child Left Behind, which in my view was (and is) harming K–12 education. But as I thought about it, I realized that No Child Left Behind was just a handy target for my more deeply rooted objections to American education. That evening I went back to my office after dinner and in about an hour laid out the main points of what became a three-part series in the *Wall Street Journal* that appeared in January 2007. The series attracted an unusual degree of attention, including many e-mails from public school teachers and college professors along the lines of "I never thought I would agree with you about anything, but this time . . ." A few weeks later, Roger Kimball suggested that I expand these themes into a book, and I realized how much I wanted to do just that.

It has been a book written in the age of the Internet. I cannot possibly remember all the scholars who responded to my e-mails requesting PDFs of their work, often helpfully suggesting other publications to go with them. But special thanks go to Jennifer Kobrin, who responded to many questions about her study of college readiness; Greg Duncan, who clarified some issues regarding the

Infant Health Development Program; David Kay, who gave me access to WordSmart's vocabulary research; Jay Greene, who walked me through the data on tax credit and voucher programs; Rick Hess, for sharing his expertise; and Chris DeMuth, for suggestions that materially improved the text. Howard Gardner cheerfully agreed to vet my description of his seven original intelligences, but he cannot be held responsible for anything else in the book. Showing him the rest of the text would have spoiled the fun for both of us.

Binky Urban found me just the right editor and Sean Desmond provided just the right editorial guidance. Catherine Cox wielded her red pen with the icy indifference to my feelings that would make her indispensable even if she weren't my treasured soul mate when she puts the red pen away.

Charles Murray
Burkittsville, Maryland
March 10, 2008

Introduction

This book calls for a transformation of American education—a transformation not just of means, but of ends. We need to change the way the schools do business. We also need to redefine educational success.

My targets are not the usual suspects. I do not inveigh against high dropout rates, low test scores, or obdurate teachers' unions. My indictment is much broader: The educational system is living a lie.

The lie is that every child can be anything he or she wants to be. No one really believes it, but we approach education's problems as if we did. We are phobic about saying out loud that children differ in their ability to learn the things that schools teach. Not only do we hate to say it, we get angry with people who do. We insist that the emperor *is* wearing clothes, beautiful clothes, and that those who say otherwise are bad people.

Call it educational romanticism. We have idealized images of the potential that children bring to the classroom and of our ability to realize that potential. When the facts get in the way, we ignore them. Try to think of the last time you saw a newspaper story about No Child Left Behind that mentioned low intellectual ability as the reason why some students don't perform at grade level. Try to think of the last article you read about young people who do not go to college that used the intellectual demands of college-level work as an explanation. I doubt if you can think of a single instance in either case. I certainly can't. The silence about differences in intellectual ability on educational topics that scream for their discussion is astonishing. It amounts to living a lie.

If the system were living a kindly lie, I would not have written this book. The lie is certainly meant kindly. Everyone wants only the best for every child. But its effects play out in the lives of young people in devastating ways. The nine-year-old who has trouble sounding out simple words and his classmate who is reading *A Tale of Two Cities* for fun sit in the same classroom day after miserable day, the one so frustrated by tasks he cannot do and the other so bored that both are near tears. The fifteen-year-old who cannot make sense of algebra but has an almost mystical knack with machines is told to stick with the college prep track, because to be a success in life he must go to college and get a BA. The twenty-year-old who knocks the top off standardized tests is still turning in rubbish on his college term papers because no one has ever taught him how to be his own toughest critic. They are all products of an educational system that cannot make itself talk openly about the implications of diverse educational limits.

And so a fog of wishful thinking, euphemisms, and well-intended egalitarianism hangs over the discussion of education, obscuring simple truths. This book is about four of them:

- Ability varies.
- Half of the children are below average.
- Too many people are going to college.

- America's future depends on how we educate the academically gifted.

The unifying theme of the chapters that follow is that we are unrealistic about students at every level of academic ability—asking too much from those at the bottom, asking the wrong things from those in the middle, and asking too little from those at the top.

The policy implications of ending educational romanticism cut in many directions. While half the children are below average, the current educational system shortchanges their ability to profit from the assets they do possess. The students on college campuses who do not belong there include many with high IQs. Those who are lucky enough to be academically gifted will play a crucial role in America's future, but the last thing we need is an educational system that pampers them. In the final chapter, I describe an educational system that embraces the simple truths.

Real Education

1

Ability Varies

The first of the simple truths is the simplest. All of us have known since our earliest memories of elementary school that abilities are real and that they vary. Whether it was a game of tag at recess or reading aloud from *Dick and Jane*, we observed that some of our classmates did better than others.

As soon as I move beyond that simplest two-word expression, *ability varies*, controversy begins. What abilities are we talking about? To what degree is ability determined by genes, to what degree by environment? Matters get even touchier as abilities of various kinds become entangled in issues of race, class, and gender.

For the moment, ignore the hot buttons. It is possible to talk about variation in ability in ways that almost everyone can accept. Laying out that common ground is the purpose of this chapter.

As a framework for talking about abilities, I will borrow from the best-known classification, Howard Gardner's multiple intelligences. In his original presentation in 1983, Gardner specified seven intelligences: bodily-kinesthetic, musical, interpersonal, intrapersonal, spatial, linguistic, and logical-mathematical. He has since expanded the list to eight (the additional one is naturalistic intelligence), with a few more candidates still in the works. I will stay with the original seven, focusing on their educational and occupational relevance.

Bodily-kinesthetic intelligence encompasses physical skills—gross motor skills, fine motor skills, and more generally, the ability to exert subtle and precise physical control over one's movements. Careers that call for good bodily-kinesthetic intelligence include athletics, the performing arts, and crafts.

Musical intelligence is what it sounds like, encompassing highly developed senses of pitch, rhythm, tones, and the ways in which they combine. People who need good musical intelligence to make their livings include musicians, singers, conductors, and composers.

Interpersonal intelligence involves interactions with others. People with high interpersonal intelligence are good at sensing others' emotions and motivations. They are empathetic, able to work effectively as part of a group, good at communicating with others, and effective at manipulating the responses of others. High interpersonal intelligence is useful for almost any career, but is especially important in occupations such as management, sales, teaching, the ministry, and the caring professions. It is vital for politicians.

Intrapersonal intelligence involves knowing oneself and being able to use that knowledge effectively. People with high intrapersonal intelligence have a realistic grasp of their own emotions, motivations, strengths, and limits. They are able to exert self-discipline and defer gratification. They can remain analytical in times of stress. Courage and prudence are parts of intrapersonal intelligence. In excess, some of the qualities that go into intrapersonal intelligence can express themselves as neuroticism or extreme introversion, and can paralyze action through overanalysis. But when those qualities remain within bounds, high intrapersonal intelligence facilitates performance in any occupation.

Spatial intelligence refers in part to the ability to visualize and mentally manipulate objects, as when an engineer holistically grasps how the parts of a mechanism interact or a chess master plays a game without looking at the board. It is possible to have high spatial intelligence in this sense even if one is blind. This is also the aspect of spatial intelligence measured in IQ tests. Gardner adds other elements to his concept of spatial intelligence, however. For example, an accomplished artist perceives things visually that escape people with ordinary spatial intelligence. A good sailor calls on spatial intelligence when he determines his boat's position by dead reckoning. Good hand-eye coordination is also an aspect of spatial intelligence. Occupations in which spatial intelligence is especially important include architecture, engineering, mathematics, the sciences, the visual arts, and crafts.

Logical-mathematical intelligence involves numbers, logic, and abstractions. By definition, high logical-mathematical intelligence means the capacity for advanced mathematics, but it also expresses itself in the ability to mount and understand complex arguments and chains of reasoning, and the ability to make subtle distinctions. Logical-mathematical intelligence is especially important in the sciences and the law, but is useful for every occupation.

Linguistic intelligence embraces everything having to do with language and the information language conveys. High linguistic intelligence includes the abilities to absorb complex written text and to express oneself precisely, eloquently, or persuasively as the situation may require. The ability to learn foreign languages easily is associated with high linguistic intelligence. Memory—the ability to store and retrieve large amounts of information at will—is part of linguistic intelligence. Linguistic intelligence is especially important for any career that involves extensive writing or speaking, but is useful for every occupation.

Howard Gardner calls these abilities intelligences to give them the status associated with the word *intelligence*. I will go in the other direction, and refrain from using *intelligence* at all, confining myself instead to *ability*. I do this partly to sidestep technical controversies about the theory of multiple intelligences that are not germane to our topic and partly because I agree with Gardner that *intelligence* has taken on a penumbra of unwarranted connotations. Intelligence traditionally understood is an ability—a very important one, but just an ability nonetheless.

Ability Not Only Varies, It Varies a Lot

The distance between low and high on all seven abilities is wide. For purposes of illustration, here are some extremes:

> *Bodily-kinesthetic*: from someone who trips over his own feet to Fred Astaire
> *Musical*: from tone-deaf to Mozart
> *Spatial*: from someone who gets lost two blocks from home to Daniel Boone
> *Linguistic*: from unable to form sentences to Shakespeare
> *Logical-mathematical*: from unable to understand cause and effect to Aristotle
> *Interpersonal*: from autism to Bill Clinton
> *Intrapersonal*: from an undisciplined narcissist to Confucius

The differences that exist in a random cross-section of the population are not as wide as these examples, but they are still wide. They consist of two types: differences in degree, and differences in kind. Bodily-kinesthetic ability offers many examples. People with a wide range of bodily-kinesthetic ability can play tennis. The difference between the way most people play tennis and the way that professionals play it is huge, but it is a difference of degree. In contrast, doing a somersault with a full twist off a pommel horse is impossible for most people, no matter how much they might practice. The difference in what they can do and what the proficient gymnast can do is one of kind.

This point needs emphasizing. Educational measures such as test scores and grades tend to make differences among schoolchildren look as though they are ones of degree when in reality some of them are differences in kind. For example, a timed math test limited to problems of addition and subtraction, administered to a random cross-section of fourth-graders, yields scores that place children along a continuum distributed in a shape resembling a bell curve. Those scores appropriately reflect differences in degree: Some fourth-graders can add and subtract faster and more accurately than others, but they are all doing the same thing and almost all children can be taught to add and subtract to some degree. The same is not true of calculus. If all children were put on a mathematics track that took them through calculus, and then were given a test of calculus problems, the resulting scores would not look like a bell curve. For a large proportion of children, the scores would not be merely low. They would be zero. Grasping calculus requires a certain level of logical-mathematical ability. Children below that level will never learn calculus, no matter how hard they study. It is a difference in kind. Not only that: The child without the logical-mathematical ability to learn calculus cannot do a wide variety of other things in mathematics that are open to the child with the requisite level of logical-mathematical ability.

The same distinction applies to linguistic ability. Reading is something that almost everyone can be taught to some degree, and scores on tests of reading achievement will form a continuum with a distribution resembling a bell curve. But if we are talking about a classroom discussion of *Macbeth* among high-school seniors at the 20th percentile and 90th percentile in linguistic ability, the difference is more accurately seen as a difference in kind than as a difference in degree. Those at the 20th percentile will completely fail to understand the text in the same way that someone at the 20th percentile of bodily-kinesthetic ability will completely fail to do a somersault with a full twist.

Many of the things that high-ability students can do are different in kind from the things that low-ability students can do. That's a fact, and the design of every aspect of education needs to keep it in mind.

The Seven Abilities Are Not Equally Valuable in Adult Life

There may be seven distinct abilities, but two and a half of them have limited relevance to success as adults. Few adults make their living in occupations that demand exceptionally high bodily-kinesthetic, musical, or spatial abilities as the indispensable requirement for excellence.

Regarding bodily-kinesthetic ability: As of 2005, the Department of Labor estimated that 12,230 Americans made their living as athletes and 16,240 as dancers. That works out to one out of every 4,600 workers. There are many more people working as athletic coaches, but their own bodily-kinesthetic ability is not nearly as important as their teaching skills.

Regarding musical ability: In 2005, 50,410 people made their living as musicians and singers, and 8,610 as music directors and composers, together representing one out of 2,200 workers. As in the case of athletic coaches, music teachers need good musical ability, but teaching skills are crucial.

Regarding spatial ability: The importance of spatial ability in adult life depends on whether we are talking about mental visualization and manipulation of objects, which is important at the highest levels of achievement among engineers, architects, and many kinds of scientists, or the broader aspects of Gardner's concept of spatial ability that encompass such things as an artist's spatial perceptions and hand-eye coordination. Except for visual artists, the latter kind of spatial abilities need to be "good enough" for certain occupations—surgery and carpentry, for example—but not necessarily exceptional. Extraordinary hand-eye coordination is not what separates the best surgeons and carpenters from the ordinary.

Bodily-kinesthetic ability, musical ability, and spatial ability contribute to important parts of our lives, and education should do what it can to develop them. But as we focus on education's core function, to prepare people for adult life, the remaining four abilities—interpersonal, intrapersonal, linguistic, and logical-mathematical—are the invaluable all-purpose tools.

Links in the Expression of the Abilities

Now we move onto contentious ground. The story goes back to 1904, when the pioneering psychologist Charles Spearman observed that it makes no difference what mental skills are being measured in a battery of tests. In every instance, the scores on all the tests in the battery are positively correlated. (A correlation is a statistic with a range of -1 to $+1$. The extremes represent perfect inverse and direct relationships, and 0 indicates no relationship at all.) Spearman hypothesized an explanation: All of the tests tap into a general mental factor, which he named g. Spearman then devised the statistical method called factor analysis to measure the degree to which test items and test batteries measure g—are "g-loaded," in the jargon. Ever since, IQ tests have been assessed according to their power to measure g accurately.

Many things about g remain controversial. Gardner's theory of multiple intelligences is involved in the controversy because Gardner argues that his seven intelligences are not only conceptually distinct, but also operationally distinct; that is, scores on the seven abilities would *not* be correlated if only our measures were good enough. Let me try to carve out a few narrow statements about g and the seven abilities that are not in empirical dispute, and then offer my interpretation of how they affect straight thinking about education. They all derive from the general observation that, using the measures that do exist, a high level of any cognitive ability has some positive statistical association with g.

Spatial Ability, Logical–Mathematical Ability, and Linguistic Ability

Of Gardner's seven abilities, these three are nearly coincident with the ones that IQ tests measure. For logical-mathematical ability and linguistic ability, there are no important operational differences between Gardner's characterization of them and the ones that the designers of IQ tests bring to their task. I must again impose caveats on spatial ability. I know of no data linking g with the qualities that enabled Daniel Boone to walk through trackless forest for months on end and still find his way home, or with the spatial apprehensions that sculptors call upon, or the spatial aspects of hand-eye coordination. But proficiency in the visualization of objects in three dimensions and the mental manipulation of them are exactly what certain subtests in the major IQ batteries calibrate.

I lump these three abilities together (two and a half, actually) because measures of them are so highly correlated with g, with the correlations usually falling in the +.7 to +.9 range, depending on the specific test battery and the population being tested. Correlations this high mean that scores on these separate abilities are interchangeable in large populations. The combination of the three constitute that thing which has been called *intelligence, mental ability, cognitive ability,* or *intellectual ability.* I will refer to the combination of the three as *academic ability.* I must emphasize that a label doesn't change the underlying nature of the construct. The three component abilities are valuable in every aspect of human life, not just education, and an IQ score by any other name is still just as g-loaded. But *academic ability* is a good label to use in a book about education. Dictionary definitions of *academic* focus on its relationship to higher education and to education that is liberal or classical rather than vocational. Linguistic, logical-mathematical, and certain spatial abilities are decisive in determining how well students can perform in courses that fit that description. So with just an occasional exception, *academic ability* it shall henceforth be.

The three components of academic ability are interchangeable in groups but not in individuals. You probably think of yourself as better in one of the components than in the other two, for example. But don't confuse such differences with lack of correlation. Successful lawyers and English professors who consider themselves dolts in math usually had SAT-Math scores that were far above what would be the average if all seventeen-year-olds took the SAT; their math scores were pedestrian only in comparison with others headed for college.

The reason to combine the three components into a single measure of academic ability such as an IQ score is that treating them separately is pointless when working with large groups. Suppose, for example, that you have a sample of 10,000 people and want to analyze the relationships of spatial, linguistic, and logical-mathematical abilities to completed years of education among adults. The three analyses will produce almost identical results—that is guaranteed by the combination of large samples and the high intercorrelations of the three components of academic ability. You lose nothing by combining the components into a single measure, and actually gain something in the form of higher reliability in your results.

Here is the distinction you should keep in mind throughout the rest of the book: For understanding *an individual child* and what that child's educational needs might be, you want as much disaggregation of the child's abilities as possible. For understanding the overall relationship of the components of academic ability to educational performance and later outcomes in life *for large groups of people,* you are better off using a combined measure.

Interpersonal and Intrapersonal Ability

Most aspects of interpersonal and intrapersonal ability have positive relationships to g, though often so small that they are inconsequential. In an ambitious meta-analysis of the relationship between measures of personality and measures of intelligence, personality traits that were significantly and positively correlated with g included social potency, achievement orientation, social closeness, extroversion, and openness to experience. An analysis of a large nationally representative sample showed significant positive relationships between measures of cognitive ability and measures of calmness, self-confidence, and maturity. These individual relationships involved correlations with IQ scores in the +.1 to +.3 range. Other meta-analyses of leadership, conscientiousness, and extraversion have found correlations with IQ scores of +.27, +.28, and +.31, respectively. More global measures of interpersonal ability and intrapersonal ability would probably show larger correlations with g—that's what happens when separate indicators with small relationships are aggregated into an index—but despite the publicity given to concepts such as emotional intelligence, measures of them have yet to gain wide scholarly acceptance.

When I first learned about them, I was surprised that *any* relationships existed between g and positive personality characteristics because my experience as an undergraduate at Harvard had led me to believe that people with extremely high IQs were, on average, pretty weird. My coauthor on *The Bell Curve*, the late Richard Herrnstein, pointed out my error. The high-IQ students who behaved oddly were conspicuous, so I noticed them. But if I had been given access to the students' admissions folders, I would have found that the majority of students with stratospheric IQs also had above-average skills in the areas that Gardner labels interpersonal and intrapersonal. No one has ever documented the common belief (which I shared) that high IQ is systematically related to dysfunctional personality characteristics.

MUSICAL ABILITY

Several studies of musical ability and g have been done, and they find a correlation of about +.3. The existence of a correlation makes sense. Raw musical talent can take a performer a long way, but Yo-Yo Ma's interpretation of a Bach suite for unaccompanied cello calls upon cognitive abilities as well, and the cognitive abilities Bach needed to write that suite are still more obvious. Memory also is important for a musical composer or performer, and memory is related to g. High achievement in music is also surely related to intrapersonal qualities such as self-discipline and perseverance, which in turn have a relationship with g.

BODILY-KINESTHETIC ABILITY

The association with g is probably smallest in the case of bodily-kinesthetic ability. I cannot be more precise than that because (to my knowledge) there is no good literature on the subject. The teams of the National Football League must think that g has some relationship to performance, because they have been administering the Wonderlic Intelligence Test to prospective draftees for years. Some teams have assigned minimum scores required for different positions, with quarterback having the highest floor. Other sports such as golf give an advantage to people who can think ahead and can accurately assess the probabilities associated with alternative choices ("Should I go for the green or lay up short of the water hazard?"). These qualities presumably create some association between sporting achievement and g, especially at the highest levels. As in the case of music, it is also surely true that high achievement in sports is related to intrapersonal qualities that are statistically related to g. Apart from the obvious roles of self-discipline and perseverance, the reason that a handful of athletes can perform at their best under the most pressure—they don't choke as ordinary people do—involves intrapersonal qualities such as emotional self-control and ability to focus despite distractions. It seems safe to assume that the sign of the relationship of g to athletic achievement is often positive within a given sport, or within a given position within a given sport, but nothing more ambitious than that.

In summary: Ability varies and it varies a lot. Four of the seven abilities are especially important in adult life. A mathematical correlation is known to exist between g and the existing operational measures of six of the seven abilities. It probably exists to a limited extent for bodily-kinesthetic ability. For the components of academic ability, the statistical association is quite strong. What does it all mean for straight thinking about education?

To me, it means that educators who proceed on the assumption that they can find some ability in which every child is above average are kidding themselves. It is not Howard Gardner's fault, but the theory of multiple intelligences has become a justification for educational romanticism. The truth that people may possess many different abilities is unthinkingly transmuted into an untruth: that everyone is good at something, and that educators can use that something to make up for other deficits.

Empirically, it is not the case that we can expect a child who is below average in one ability to have a full and equal chance of being above average in the other abilities. Those chances are constrained by the observed relationship that links the abilities. In the case of bodily-kinesthetic and musical ability, those relationships are small enough that they don't matter much. In the case of interpersonal and intrapersonal ability, the relationships are somewhat larger, and they have to be recognized. In the case of the three components of academic ability, the relationships are extremely close. It is a classic example of life not being fair. The child who knows all the answers in math class has a high probability of reading above grade level as well and, what's more, a higher than average chance of being industrious and determined. Conversely, children who are at the bottom of the math class usually have trouble with reading as well, and also have a higher than average chance of showing problems with thinking ahead and disciplining themselves.

Many exceptions exist, of course, and educational practice at any good school should ensure that exceptions are identified. But it is one thing to be on the lookout for exceptions, and another to talk breezily about multiple intelligences and how different children learn in different but equally valid ways, and pretend that if only we tap the special abilities that reside in every child, everything will work out. Ability varies. For any given ability, the population forms a continuum that goes from very low to very high. The core abilities that dominate academic success vary together. Schools that ignore those realities are doing a disservice to all their students.

Half of the Children Are
Below Average

We do not live in Lake Wobegon. For each of the seven abilities, half of the children are below average. The topic of this chapter is what it means to be below average—below the median, if you prefer—and the consequent implications for education.

Just about every reader understands what *below average* means for some of the abilities. Either you know people who fit the bill or you fit it yourself. For example, about half of you are below average in bodily-kinesthetic ability. You were picked late when choosing teams for playground games. You were not good enough even to try out for the varsity. Perhaps you liked playing some sports, but you just couldn't make your body do the things some of your friends could do. If not true of you, these statements are probably true of people you know.

Many of you are below average in certain kinds of spatial ability. If you had to take shop class, you couldn't make the band saw cut the wood into exactly the right shape. Everything you nailed or glued together was a little bit off. Or perhaps you go to art museums and cannot figure out why some people spend so long looking at one painting. What more is there to see after the first glance? If not true of you, these statements are probably true of people you know.

Many of you are below average in musical ability. You cannot carry a tune very well and never got the hang of the instrument your parents made you practice when you were a child. If you learned to read music, it was like a poorly learned foreign language—your linguistic ability let you memorize the grammar and decode the symbols, but the poetry escaped you. You learned the technical difference between C major and F major, but you couldn't listen to compositions and recognize the difference, and you never understood why someone would choose to compose in one key rather than another. If not true of you, these statements are probably true of people you know.

Many of you are below average in certain interpersonal skills. Perhaps you are painfully shy. Perhaps you are socially abrasive, don't read body language well, or find it hard to empathize. If not true of you, these statements are probably true of people you know.

Many of you are below average in certain intrapersonal abilities. Perhaps you procrastinate. Perhaps you are careless, fearful, or narcissistic. Perhaps you choke under pressure, occasionally break your word, or give up if the going gets tough. If not true of you, these statements are probably true of people you know.

In short, just about every reader understands from personal and vicarious life experiences what *below average* means for bodily-kinesthetic, musical, interpersonal, and intrapersonal ability, and for the aspects of spatial ability associated with hand-eye coordination and visual apprehension. You may think you also know what *below average* means for linguistic ability, logical-mathematical ability, and spatial abilities associated with mental visualization because you know you are better at some of these intellectual tasks than at others. But here you are probably mistaken. It is safe to say that a majority of readers have little experience with what it means to be below average in any of the components of academic ability.

The first basis for this statement is that I know you have reached the second chapter of a nonfiction book on a public policy issue, which means you are probably well above average in academic ability—not because getting to the second chapter of this book requires that you be especially bright, but because people with below-average academic ability hardly ever choose to read books like this.

The second basis for my statement is the nature of cognitive segregation. Do any of these statements apply to you?

- You grew up in an upper-middle-class or affluent neighborhood.
- You grew up in a neighborhood of middle-income people in high-IQ professions (e.g., a neighborhood filled with college faculty).
- You attended a selective school, public or private.

If any of these statements applies, the school you attended contained few students in the lower half of the intellectual range. Instead, the average student at your school was far above average relative to all Americans, and the students at the bottom of the class were around the national average.

If you went to a public school, you can check out the accuracy of that statement for yourself. A number of websites show test data by school. Get the scores for your school and compare them with the state mean. Since your comparison group is the national population, you should factor in the national ranking of your state, but just looking at the difference in scores between your school and the state average will give you a good sense of how exceptional your school was. As a rule of thumb, you may assume that the average student in schools that draw from upper-middle-class neighborhoods is between roughly the 75th and 90th percentile of all Americans, and that only 10 to 20 percent of the children in that student body are anywhere below the national average. The bottom third of the national distribution is almost completely unrepresented. If you went to a selective private or public school, the distribution of academic ability was even more severely skewed; even students at the bottom of the class in such schools are often above the national average.

Suppose you answered *no* to all three questions, probably because you lived in a town where a single high school served the entire population and the town itself included a broad socioeconomic spread. Your classmates were a fair representation of the entire national distribution of academic ability. Does this mean that you were likely to have close friends who were below average in academic ability?

No, because cognitive self-segregation occurred within your school. You may have entered tracked reading and math classes as early as elementary school. But whether or not your school system formally tracked, students with different levels of academic ability began to take different courses as soon as choice became available in middle school and high school. Hardly any students below the national average in academic ability were in the science, math, and foreign-language courses you elected to take, and probably none tried to take the honors courses.

Now add to the mix the universal tendency of people to make friends based on similar interests. Sometimes these interests can cut across different levels of academic ability, as in varsity sports or the band. But the more important the intellectual component of the activity—as in the case of the debate team, student newspaper, drama department, or computer club—the less likely it is that students with below-average academic ability become involved.

Combine the various forces, and the net effect is powerful and nearly universal. No matter where you went to school, the fact that you are reading this book and grew up in the last half of the twentieth century means the chances are small that you ever had a close, long-term relationship with someone who was below average in academic ability. Asked to describe the things that a person with average academic ability can do, you will probably describe a person who is actually above average.

Therefore the first task is to understand what *below average* means when it comes to academic ability. The best way is to show the kinds of test questions that people with below-average academic ability have trouble answering. I take them from items that have been used on the National Assessment of Educational Progress (NAEP, pronounced "nape"), the program used by the federal Department of Education since 1971 to track student accomplishment. It is administered periodically to nationally representative samples of students in the fourth, eighth, and twelfth grades. It is a test designed to test what has been learned, not academic ability, and is regarded as the gold standard for measuring academic achievement at the elementary and secondary levels. The examples I will use are from the test for eighth-graders. I begin with a simple mathematics problem:

Example 1. *There were 90 employees in a company last year. This year the number of employees increased by 10 percent. How many employees are in the company this year?*

(A) 9   (B) 81   (C) 91   (D) 99   (E) 100

By eighth grade, it would seem that almost everyone should be able to handle a question like this. Children are taught to divide and to calculate percentages in elementary school. Dividing by ten is the easiest form of division. Dividing a whole number by ten is easier yet. Adding a one-digit number (9) to a two-digit number (90) is elementary.

It is a problem based on a simple mathematical concept, using simple arithmetic, requiring a simple logical interpolation to get the right answer. It is an excellent example for starting to think about what *below average* means in mathematics—because 62 percent of eighth-graders got this item wrong. It does not represent an item that below-average students could not do, but one that many above-average students could not do. Actually, more than 62 percent did not know the answer, because some of them got the right answer by guessing. To estimate the total percentage of students who did not know the right answer on a question with x alternatives, multiply the total percentage of students who chose one of the wrong alternatives by $x/(x-1)$. There are more sophisticated ways, but this one is close enough for our purposes. In this case, the estimated proportion of students who did not know the right answer is $(.62 \times 5/4)$, or 77.5 percent.

Now consider some items that more specifically identify what it means to be below average in math as an eighth-grader.

Example 2. *Amanda wants to paint each face of a cube a different color. How many colors will she need?*

(A) Three   (B) Four   (C) Six   (D) Eight

Twenty percent of eighth-graders did not choose C. Approximately 27 percent did not know the right answer.

Example 3. *How many of the angles in this triangle are smaller than a right angle?*

(A) None   (B) One   (C) Two   (D) Three

Thirty-one percent of eighth-graders did not choose C. Approximately 41 percent did not know the right answer.

Example 4. *What is 4 hundredths written in decimal notation?*

(A) 0.004 (B) 0.04 (C) 0.400 (D) 4.00 (E) 400.0

Thirty-two percent of eighth-graders did not choose B. Approximately 40 percent did not know the right answer.

Now consider what it means to be in the lower half of the distribution on NAEP's reading test for eighth-graders. The first example is taken from questions about an advertisement for placing classified ads. In the advertisement, a large headline in bold type says

"3 DAYS FOR FREE." To the right of the headline is a box containing the words "SPECIAL OFFER. ITEMS MUST BE $25 OR LESS." A sentence of text following the headline and box repeats this information. Students are subsequently given this multiple-choice item:

Example 5. *If you want to place a free ad, your items must be*

(A) **sold within five days**
(B) **priced at $25 or less**
(C) **in good condition**
(D) **inspected by the editor**

Thirty-four percent of eighth-graders failed to choose B. Approximately 45 percent did not know the right answer.

The next example is based on a pamphlet used by an urban public transportation system to describe its services. The pamphlet has a series of large, conspicuous subheads, each followed by a text block. One subhead is "Transfers." The first sentence in the text block is "Metrobus transfers are free and valid for unlimited Metrobus connections—including round-trips and stopovers—during the two-hour period shown on the transfer." Students were subsequently asked to answer this item:

Example 6. *According to the guide, how long are Metrobus transfers valid?*

(A) **Two hours**
(B) **All day**
(C) **One week**
(D) **Twenty-eight days**

Forty-five percent of eighth-graders did not choose A. Approximately 60 percent did not know the right answer.

The last example is taken from the questions that eighth-graders were asked about a passage describing the history of the Anasazi tribe. The question refers to these lines in the passage:

> The Anasazi made beautiful pottery, turquoise jewelry, fine sashes of woven hair, and baskets woven tightly enough to hold water. They lived by hunting and by growing corn and squash. Their way of life went on peacefully for several hundred years. Then around 1200 AD something strange happened, for which the reasons are not quite clear.

Here is the item:

Example 7. *The Anasazi's life before 1200 AD was portrayed by the author as being*

      (A) dangerous and warlike
      (B) busy and exciting
      (C) difficult and dreary
      (D) productive and peaceful

Forty-one percent of eighth-graders did not choose D. Approximately 55 percent did not know the right answer.

The schools are the usual scapegoats for results like these. But how much can they be blamed that three-quarters of eighth-graders did not know the answer to the question about percentages in Example 1? Ask those same children what 10 percent of 90 is, and you will find that many if not most of them learned enough multiplication and percentages to give you the answer. Ask them what 90 plus 9 is, and you will find that almost all of them can add those numbers. What they failed to do was put everything together—to realize that first they had to take 10 percent of 90, and then add the result to 90. This logical step does not lend itself to being taught in the same way that the rules for addition and multiplication can be taught. A teacher can explain the logical step for this particular example. That's why teaching to the test can work: If teachers know that the state competency test will include one item of this particular type, they can drill the students and raise the proportion that answer it correctly. But if the test uses a new context and puts a different twist on the problem (for example, asking students to calculate a percentage reduction instead of a percentage increase), it is up to the students to generalize their knowledge, and that calls upon logical-mathematical ability.

It is even harder to blame the schools for mistakes in the other three math examples about cubes, right angles, and decimal notation. All eighth-graders have encountered cubes, right angles, and decimal notation in the classroom before eighth grade. Before you conclude that the schools just didn't do a good enough job of presenting the material, talk to elementary and middle school teachers about their experiences trying to teach children who are well below average in logical-mathematical ability. Yes, given time, you may be able to get such a child to understand a right angle, but a few days later you have to explain it anew, and a few days after that the same thing; the understanding is lost again. The concept of a right angle will not stick. Similarly, the concept of decimal notation may be grasped for the duration of the tutoring, but it does not stick. A few days later, given a fresh exercise using decimal notation, the student will miss every question because the concept of decimal notation is beyond the capacity of that child to absorb and retain. Could such a child absorb and retain the concept of decimal notation if the teacher is given unlimited time and resources? Sometimes yes, sometimes no, but the investment of time must be so large that it cannot possibly be generalized to the whole curriculum. Limits on logical-mathematical ability translate into limits on how much math a large number of children can learn no matter what the school system does.

The three reading examples illustrate another aspect of the ceiling that faces students in the lower half of the distribution. Literacy requires not just the linguistic ability to decode individual words, but also the logical-mathematical ability to infer, deduce, and interpolate. Of the roughly 45 percent of students who did not know the price of items in a free ad, it is safe to assume that almost all could read the words *days, for, free, special, offer, must, be, or,* and *less.* Presumably all of them understood the symbols 3 and $25. They did not miss the item because they could not decode words, but because they could not interpret how the headline related to the information in the box—a task so simple that it does not seem like interpretation until one stops to think about it.

Illiteracy strictly defined cannot explain the roughly 60 percent who could not figure out how long Metrobus transfers are valid. Here's the sentence again, following immediately after the conspicuous heading "Transfers": "Metrobus transfers are free and valid for unlimited Metrobus connections—including round-trips and stopovers—during the two-hour period shown on the transfer." Neither the vocabulary nor the sentence construction should pose a problem for a child with even modest reading ability. What prevented a majority of students from knowing the answer? A major part of the reason was that the students couldn't find the information in the brochure. Finding information in a pamphlet when time is limited is not just a matter of reading words, but of using search strategies:

scanning the headings to get a sense of content (the intellectual aspects of spatial ability come into this), matching the material you're looking for to the headings (logical-mathematical ability), then focusing on the text connected to the heading (linguistic ability). It is a task beyond the capability of many children. A teacher can show them how to do it by rote for this particular pamphlet, but it is hard to teach them how to do it again when faced with another pamphlet on another topic with a different format.

Why weren't students able to answer the question about the Anasazi? The question mentions 1200 AD—a specific, easy-to-find key that occurs only once in the passage. The sentence immediately preceding "1200 AD" in the passage uses exactly the same word— *peaceful*—as one of the pairs of words in alternative D. That alone should be enough to lead a student to choose D if he were in doubt about the right answer. The passage's previous sentence talks about the Anasazi making things, obviously related to the meaning of *productive*. And just to make the question even easier, none of the other options used difficult vocabulary or a tricky distractor. Answering the question about the Anasazi would seem to be a no-brainer. But 41 percent nonetheless chose the wrong answer, and about 14 percent got it right only by guessing, because none of those steps I just described is easy for someone well into the lower half of academic ability. Picking up on "1200 AD" as the place to start looking for the answer involves inference. To realize upon reading "Then around 1200 AD . . ." that the preceding text is the place to look for the answer is a logical-mathematical task as well as a linguistic one, drawing an implication from the time sequence denoted by the use of *then*. Picking out the verb *made* and seeing its relationship to *productivity* is another inference. Psychologist Edward L. Thorndike, writing in 1917, put the intimate interconnection between reading comprehension and academic ability as well as anyone since: "The mind is assailed as it were by every word in the paragraph. It must select, repress, soften, emphasize, correlate and organize, all under the influence of the right mental set or purpose or demand."

Put yourself once again in the position of the teacher. How does one teach a child to make inferential leaps? Drilling in vocabulary will not help. Diagramming sentences will not help. The skills that the child must master do not involve learning words or the mechanics of reading, but putting two and two together in novel settings. It is appropriate to blame the schools when it is reported that, for example, more than half of eighth-graders do not know who was president during World War II or that about two-thirds do not know why the Bill of Rights was added to the Constitution (real examples from NAEP). Lack of academic ability does not account for those astonishing percentages. Students with a wide range of academic ability can remember unadorned facts. But the reading and math examples are different. Part of the blame for the high percentages of wrong answers may be assigned to schools, but not nearly all of it. Many of the wrong answers reflect nothing more complicated than low academic ability.

Schools Have No Choice But to Leave Many Children Behind

For five of the seven abilities, the educational system has realistic expectations and behaves sensibly. Children with below-average bodily-kinesthetic ability have to take PE with everybody else, but no one tries to make them into good athletes. Children with below-average musical ability are usually exposed to music classes in elementary school, but they are allowed to drop out thereafter. Children with below-average spatial skills are usually exposed to art classes in elementary school, and in middle school may be exposed to a year of shop, but they are allowed to drop out thereafter. When it comes to interpersonal skills, good teachers will try to give some protection to children who are especially shy and restrain children who are especially aggressive, but the typical school does not undertake to transform their students' interpersonal skills for the better, and reasonable parents do not expect them to do so. Children with below-average intrapersonal skills can be helped by a school that reinforces good study habits and enforces appropriate social behavior in the halls and classroom, but everyone accepts that the child's inherited characteristics and socialization at home in the preschool years limit what the school can accomplish.

Only for linguistic and logical-mathematical ability are we told that we can expect everyone to do well. Neither politicians nor school boards will publicly accept the reality that I tried to illustrate with the questions from NAEP. Children in the lower half of the distribution are just not smart enough to read or calculate at a level of fluency that most of the rest of us take for granted. Children still lower in the distribution of linguistic and logical-mathematical ability—the bottom third of the distribution is a rough demarcation of the group I am talking about—are just not smart enough to become literate or numerate in more than a rudimentary sense.

Just not smart enough: It is a phrase that we all use in conversation, we all know what it means, and it has to be made available once again to discussions about educational policy. Some children are just not smart enough to succeed on a conventional academic track. Recognition of this truth does not mean callousness or indifference. It does not mean spending less effort on the education of some children than of others. But it does mean that we must jettison glib rhetoric that makes us feel good. No more talk about leaving no child behind. No more accusations that to be realistic is "the soft bigotry of low expectations." No more celebrations of attempts to "challenge" students without regard to their ability.

To get to that point—to accept that it is okay to think in terms of what a child may reasonably be expected to accomplish—I think it is appropriate to personalize the issue. Let us forget for a moment about children who are below average in academic ability and think instead about ourselves and what it is reasonable to expect of us. The proposition on the table is that *our best educational experiences were ones in which adults insisted we could do better when in fact we* could *do better; our worst educational experiences were ones in which adults insisted we could do better when in fact we* could not *do better.*

The first half of the proposition refers to the essence of what good teachers do, and I assume that all of us who have had good teachers can tell similar stories. Sometimes the teacher will have drawn out our best with encouragement, sometimes with criticism, sometimes by instruction, sometimes by example. But, by definition, the common denominator in all those memories will be that we, the students, were *able* to do better than we had realized we could.

Now take up the negative side of my proposition. Think of a time when you were a child and some smiling, well-meaning person in authority said "You can do it if you try," and you knew you couldn't. I will go first. I was eight or nine years old, it was Little League, it was the last inning, the Bruins were behind, and I (usually a bench-warmer) was coming to bat. Inexplicably, the coach chose this moment to go up and down the bench assuring everyone that I, statistically the worst hitter not just on the Bruins but in my town's entire Little League, would get a hit and win the game. More than half a century later, the memory of going up to the plate after that pep talk and (of course) striking out is seared into my psyche.

Now it's your turn. Whatever painful experience comes to mind, it surely has something in common with mine. When your smiling, well-meaning person in authority said, "You can do it if you try," *and you knew it was not true,* the well-meaning person was not raising your self-esteem. Not getting you to find untapped resources within you. He was humiliating you.

Now imagine having substantial intellectual shortcomings. It is in the nature of any school system that your shortcomings will first become humiliatingly public to your classmates when you are about six years old, and that you will have to live with that kind of humiliation until you leave school. There's no way to avoid it completely. If you are in a school that tracks by ability, you will know you are in the class for dummies. If you are in a school that doesn't track, you will be the kid who doesn't know the answer when the teacher calls on you, or the kid on whom the teacher never calls because you won't know the answer (and everybody knows why the teacher never calls on you). But at least the schools can avoid making it worse.

This is not a call for woolly-headed niceness. It is a good thing for parents and teachers to encourage children to try hard. It is a good thing to teach children that they should not give up easily. It is better to push a child farther than he can go (occasionally) than not to push at all. But one of the responsibilities of parents and teachers is to appraise the abilities that a child brings to a task. One of the most irresponsible trends in modern education has been the reduction in rigorous, systematic assessment of the abilities of all the students in their care. To demand that students meet standards that have been set without regard to their academic ability is wrong and cruel to the children who are unable to meet those standards.

When I say that schools have no choice but to leave some children behind, I do not mean that the schools have no choice but to neglect them. Every student should have full opportunity to learn as much as he can learn. Rather, I mean that even the best schools will inevitably have students who do not perform at grade level. How many merely depends on how ambitiously *grade level* is defined. Make it easy enough, and everyone who is not clinically retarded can be at grade level. Define *grade level* the way that the Bronx High School of Science does, and hardly anyone will be at grade level. If you define *grade level* as the tasks that someone of average academic ability can be taught to do, then the proportion of students who are not at grade level will be approximately 50 percent. If you define *grade level* as the tasks that someone in the top two-thirds of the distribution of academic ability can be taught to do, then the proportion of students who are not at grade level will be approximately 33 percent. In large groups of children, academic achievement is tied to academic ability. No pedagogical strategy, no improvement in teacher training, no increase in homework, no reduction in class size can break that connection.

There are three plausible ways to argue that I am wrong: The measure of academic ability is invalid. We can raise academic ability. The schools are so bad that low-ability students can learn a lot more even if their ability is unchanged. Responding to the first two can be done briskly (the chapter notes guide the curious to more details). The third one requires more explaining.

"The Measure of Academic Ability Is Invalid"

The standard measure of academic ability is an IQ score, or the score on some other highly *g*-loaded test. There are lots of things to argue about when the topic is IQ as a measure of intelligence, but that IQ scores are related to educational achievement is not one of them. The question here is not whether the thing-that-IQ-tests-measure is intelligence, but whether it is predictive of academic achievement. In practical terms, does knowing the IQ score of a first-grader tell you much about how well that child will do in school? That question is probably the most thoroughly explored topic in psychometrics (*Psychological Abstracts* already listed more than 11,000 citations of studies on the relationship of IQ scores to educational achievement as of a decade ago).

Briefly, the correlation coefficient of IQ test scores with achievement test scores is usually about +.5 to +.7 on its scale of −1 (a perfect inverse relationship) to +1 (a perfect positive relationship). That relationship is driven by the general mental factor *g*, which usually accounts for 80 to 90 percent of the predictable variance in scholastic performance. Furthermore, there is no known way to measure learning ability that captures qualities IQ scores do not. Psychometricians have attempted to measure learning ability independently of IQ, but when the data are analyzed it turns out that the measures of learning ability are so intertwined with the abilities measured by IQ tests that they serve no independent purpose.

IQ scores are not infallible. If an individual child has a low IQ score, it is appropriate to consider the possibility that the score is misleading. But the hypothesis must be falsifiable. The student can be retested with another instrument. Teachers can be interviewed about indications that the student performs better in their classrooms than he tests. But one must do more than assert that test results cannot be trusted or that teachers are not recognizing the student's potential. If test results tell a consistent story, and if those results are consistent with the student's classroom functioning, someone who has the child's best interests at heart must deal with that information. Continuing to insist that the child can do better if child and teachers try harder requires some sort of objective basis, not blind faith.

When we turn from individual scores to groups of children, the statistics on predictive validity mean that IQ scores will reliably indicate the limits of achievement for students in the lower half, bottom third, or bottom decile of the distribution. In a larger sense, however, test scores are not the point. Even if no test is administered, 50 percent of the children *are* below average, 33 percent *are* in the bottom third, and 10 percent *are* in the bottom decile. There is no getting around it.

"We Can Raise Academic Ability"

Now we come to a sensitive topic, our capacity to change underlying academic ability—in terms of tests, our capacity to raise IQ scores. But sensitive as it is, I propose that the following sentence is as uncontroversially true, scientifically, as the truth that half of the children are below average: *The most we know how to do with outside interventions is to make children who are well below average a little less below average.*

First, a few things that are not part of that truth. Environment plays a major role in the way that all of the abilities develop. Genes are not even close to being everything. Regarding IQ specifically, a total change in environment—adoption at birth provides the best evidence—can produce demonstrable increases in IQ scores. Living in persistent poverty and other kinds of severe socioeconomic disadvantage can depress scores. Furthermore, important evidence has been found for the plasticity of certain mental processes, especially during infancy and early childhood. We have reason to hope that, sometime in the future, technologies for early intervention that produce dramatic and permanent change will be developed. For that matter, the future will eventually bring technologies for manipulating genes that achieve the same end.

Second, small changes in intellectual ability that are educationally insignificant in individuals can produce important social benefits when they occur in large numbers. In *The Bell Curve*, Richard Herrnstein and I used the observed statistical relationship of IQ to various social phenomena to calculate the implied effects if the national IQ mean went from 100 to 103. The implied effects included reductions of 25 percent in the poverty rate, 18 percent in welfare recipiency, 15 percent in nonmarital births, and 12 percent in low-weight births. There was also a large implied educational effect: a decrease of 25 percent in high school dropouts. Statistical relationships do not necessarily mean that changes like these would occur in reality, but the potential exists for a small average increase in IQ to create significant outcomes.

It remains true, however, that small differences in IQ scores mean little when you are thinking in terms of specific children. Famed psychometrician Arthur Jensen has been known to say that he wouldn't pay five cents to raise his IQ five points. I will not go that far (five cents is within my price range), but his underlying point is correct. If two second-graders have IQs of 86 and 91, differences in their inter-personal ability and intrapersonal ability could have far greater impact on their academic performance than the five-point IQ differ-ence. Call it the Las Vegas Paradox. Imagine that you are permitted a one-time $1,000 bet at a Las Vegas craps table, and you make the bet that gives the house the smallest edge. It is called a pass line bet, and it gives the house a mere 1.4 percent advantage. Your chances are effectively fifty-fifty. From a practical standpoint, it would be foolish for either you or the casino to go into a single bet thinking of the odds in any other way. But if a hundred million people step to the table and make the same single $1,000 bet, the casino will make a lot of money. Each of our lives represents our single bet. A five-point IQ edge that one child has over another is meaningless in predicting the differences in the unique life that each of them has to live. Increase the IQ of a hundred million people by five points, and the effects of the difference can mean a lot to society.

Now to the story of attempts to raise IQ scores. We have no evi-dence at all that we know how to produce lasting increases in IQ scores after children reach school. All the data about the trajectory of IQ scores over the life span indicate that they stabilize around ages six to ten and typically remain unchanged until old age. The only targeted attempt to raise IQ scores for school-age children occurred in Venezuela in the early 1980s. The result was an increase in the range of 3 to 16 percentile points on the exit test, but it was never followed up to see if the increase lasted, nor is there any collateral evidence for an increase in academic achievement. It is known that coaching for the SAT can raise scores, but again we have no evidence that academic abil-ity has increased along with the test score, nor any evidence that even a simple increase in test-taking ability lasts for more than a few months.

EXPRESSING TEST SCORE CHANGES

When psychometricians talk about changes in test scores, they express them in terms of the standard deviation, a statistical yardstick that has many advantages. Being easily understood is not one of them, however, so I will use *percentile points* instead. For example, an increase of 10 percentile points means that someone who had been at the 30th percentile of students has risen to the 40th percentile of students.

You should be aware of a problem with percentile points: A percentile point gets wider as it moves toward the extremes. For example, if you raise your SAT score from 500 to 600, a hundred-point gain, you have gone from the 50th to the 84th percentile—your score has risen 34 percentile points. If you raise it from 700 to 800, you again have raised your score by a hundred points, but by only a little more than 2 percentile points, from the 97.7th to the 99.9th percentiles. None of the changes in test scores that I discuss involve changes at the extremes, or comparisons of two groups at widely differing places on the bell curve, so the use of percentile points as the measure here does not cause significant distortion. But, as a rule, approach the percentile-point measure cautiously.

Most people who have tried to raise IQ have reasonably assumed that the best time to do it is in the preschool years. During the height of the optimism about the potential effects of social programs during the last half of the 1960s and throughout the 1970s, many aggressive attempts were made to raise IQ using intensive preschool interventions, not to mention the nationwide, federally funded Head Start. Many of the programs were haphazardly or tendentiously evaluated, but enough good studies came out of this period to enable an academic group called the Consortium of Longitudinal Studies to conduct a comparative analysis of eleven of the best preschool interventions. The Consortium found that they produced an average short-term gain of about 17 percentile points relative to a control group. This gain fell off to about 7 percentile points after three years, a trivial change in any substantive sense. The Consortium's bottom line was that "the effect of early education on intelligence test scores was not permanent."

The Consortium's studies did not include the most ambitious and well publicized of the preschool programs, the Abecedarian Project, which provided intensive cognitive enrichment activities for children from severely disadvantaged backgrounds from the age of one month to five years. Its early results were apparently spectacular, with the experimental children scoring near or above the national mean on cognitive tests while the control children scored as much as 30 percentile points lower. But at the most recent follow-up at age twenty-one, the mean IQs of the experimental group and the control group put them at the 25th and 16th percentiles respectively, about the same difference that the Consortium found for the other attempts to raise IQ.

If we accept the results at age twenty-one at face value, the Abecedarian Project produced a large enough difference that it is socially worthwhile if it could be produced on a large scale, for the reasons I discussed earlier. In reality, the findings must be treated cautiously—the conduct of the Abecedarian Project and its evaluation has been the subject of controversy for twenty years. But the relevant point here is that everyone remained so far below average. Being at the 25th percentile is better than being at the 16th percentile, but it is a distinction without a difference for the life prospects of an individual.

We now have better data than the Abecedarian Project could provide about the limits of the Abecedarian approach. In the mid-1980s, when the Abecedarian Project looked as if it might have produced dramatic improvements in cognitive functioning, a new project using the Abecdecarian approach began. It was called the Infant Health and Development Program (IHDP), and selected its sample from premature low-birth-weight babies. Whereas the Abecedarian Project had just 57 children in the experimental group, IHDP had 377, along with 608 in a control group—the only intensive preschool intervention with both a randomized experimental design and a large sample. Like Abecedarian, IHDP produced results at ages two and three that were encouraging, showing significant differences in cognitive scores favoring the experimental group. At age five, how-ever, those differences had disappeared for the sample as a whole. A subsequent follow-up at age eighteen similarly failed to show any dif-ferences between the experimental and control groups. The advocates of the project emphasize that the heavier babies (with birth weights of 2,001–2,500 grams) showed higher cognitive scores than the control group. By age eighteen, those differences amounted to an advantage for the experimentals of 4 and 10 percentile points on the two tests of academic ability. On the other hand, experimental subjects who had weighed 2,000 grams or less had scores that were 5 and 6 percentile points *lower* than the controls on the same tests, and there were twice as many of them as the heavier babies. Result: no difference at all for the sample as a whole. Since no one associated with the program pre-dicted a priori that the Abecedarian approach would not work with lighter babies but would work with heavier ones, the parsimonious interpretation is that IHDP had no effect on cognitive functioning. If the gains for the heavier babies are accepted at face value, they are the same size as those of the Abecedarian and Consortium evaluations, and fall in the category of an effect that would be socially significant for large groups and educationally trivial for individuals.

The bottom line: Maybe we can move children from far below average intellectually to somewhat less below average. Nobody claims that any project anywhere has proved anything more than that.

"The Schools Are So Bad That Even Low-Ability Students Can Learn a Lot More Than They Learn Now"

We arrive now at the heart of the educational romanticism that pervades American education. As I write, the nation is entering the seventh year of the No Child Left Behind Act (NCLB), predicated on the belief that all children can perform at grade level, and is in the fifth decade of massive federal programs in education predicated on the broader belief that the academic achievement of American students from disadvantaged families can be raised substantially.

One source of the romanticism is the belief that American schools are so bad that there's lots of room for improvement for all students, including those in the lower half of the distribution. The purpose of the pages that follow is to present evidence that this belief is incorrect. The changes we can expect in academic achievement in the lower half of the ability distribution are marginal, no matter what educational reforms are introduced.

A Brief History of Changes in Academic Achievement Among the Below-Average

There is a period in the history of every developed country during which children who are below average in their underlying academic ability made a great leap forward in their academic achievement: when they started to go to school. In the United States, the biggest

jump probably occurred between 1900 and 1950. When the twentieth century began, about a quarter of all adults had not reached fifth
grade and half had not reached eighth grade. By 1940, the first year
when such data are available, 95 percent of American children ages
seven to thirteen were enrolled in school. By 1951, the percentage
still in school at ages seven to thirteen had reached 99 percent, where
it has remained ever since. We cannot be precise about the increase in
academic achivement, but there is a qualitative difference between
being completely illiterate and even semiliterate, or between not
recognizing numbers and being able to do simple arithmetic. That
progress comes with the establishment of universal K–8 schooling.

After universal education is in place, improvements are slower
and smaller. In the United States, we began to get a consistent series
of measures from NAEP's Long-Term Trend Study starting with
the 1971 test for reading and the 1973 test for math. The most recent
Long-Term Trend Study scores come from 2004.

On the mathematics test, scores increased substantially for both
fourth- and eighth-graders, and modestly for twelfth-graders. Furthermore, these gains were largest among students in the lower half
of the distribution—good news. In fact, buried in the Long-Term
Trend Study data are a few gains that are genuinely big. For
example, fourth-graders at the 25th percentile in 2004 were getting
math scores that would have put them at the 50th percentile in 1978.
Even the twelfth-graders' more modest improvements were not trivial. Twelfth-graders who were at the 25th percentile in 2004 were
getting math scores that would have put them at about the 35th
percentile in 1978.

This doesn't mean that the kind of student who could only add and
subtract in 1978 was doing algebra in 2004. Given the way NAEP

measures math achievement, scores can go up without the kids having learned how to do any more math than they already knew. If this sounds impossible, think back to our examples involving the cube and the right angle. They do not measure the ability to do actual mathematics; they just measure familiarity with concepts. There are many such items in NAEP's mathematics test. Furthermore, the items that do involve actual mathematics are weighted toward problems that assess the student's ability to "use math in context," in the jargon, which means that they often require nothing but arithmetic using whole numbers. When the Brown Center for Education Policy analyzed such items on NAEP's math test they discovered that they required math that had usually been taught by the middle of third grade—*in the test for eighth-graders.* The Brown Center concluded that "NAEP pays scant attention to computation skills, knowledge and use of fractions, decimals, and percents, or algebra beyond the rudimentary topics that are found in the first chapter of a good algebra text. In sum, we know that students are getting better at some aspects of math. But we do not know how American students are doing on other critical topics, including topics that mathematicians and others believe lay the foundation for the study of advanced mathematics."

In reading, nothing much has changed for more than a quarter of a century. There was slight improvement among fourth-graders in the 1970s, but their scores improved by just four points from 1980 to 2004. For eighth-graders and twelfth-graders, reading scores in 1980 and 2004 were within a point of each other.

The bottom line: among high school graduates, some improvement in math since the 1970s, concentrated in simple mathematical concepts and operations, and no improvement in reading. It is not a record that gives reason for optimism about another great leap forward unless the schools have been so uniformly terrible during the thirty-seven years since NAEP began that there is still a lot of room for improvement. Educational romantics assume that to be the case. But that assumption runs up against three reality tests: the Coleman Report, the evaluations of Title I, and the results of No Child Left Behind.

THE COLEMAN REPORT

The Coleman Report, named after sociologist James Coleman who led the study, responded to a mandate in the 1964 Civil Rights Act to assess the effects of inequality of educational opportunity on student achievement. The magnitude of the effort remains unmatched by anything done since. The sample for the study included 645,000 students nationwide. Data were collected not only about the students' personal school histories, but also about their parents' socioeconomic backgrounds, their neighborhoods, the curricula and facilities of their schools, and the qualifications of the teachers within those schools.

Before Coleman began his work, everybody (including Coleman) thought that the study would document a relationship between the quality of schools and the academic achievement of the students in those schools. Any other result seemed impossible. To everyone's shock, the Coleman Report instead found that the quality of schools explains almost nothing about differences in academic achievement. Measures such as the credentials of the teachers, the curriculum, the extensiveness and newness of physical facilities, money spent per student—none of the things that people assumed were important in explaining educational achievement were important in fact. Family background was far and away the most important factor in determining student achievement.

The Coleman Report came under intense fire, but reanalyses of the Coleman data and the collection of new data over many years supported the core finding: The quality of public schools just doesn't make much difference in student achievement. This is not to say that a good teacher cannot make a big difference in an individual student's school experience, or that parents should not care about the quality of their child's school. Rather, the Coleman Report says that the mean scores of large numbers of students are not sensitive to the differences that exist in the real world. Once a school reaches mediocrity, a lot of the slack has been taken out of the room for improvement in academic achievement for the average student. The mediocre school typically maintains a reasonably good learning environment. The mediocre school offers a standard range of courses taught with standard textbooks. An excellent school with excellent teachers will do better with that material than a mediocre school with mediocre teachers, but the average effect on test scores will not be dramatic.

Title I

After figuring out how to explain away the Coleman Report, an educational romantic must confront the accumulated evaluations of Title I. Title I is the most famous section of the Elementary and Secondary Education Act of 1965 (which Congress passed without bothering to wait for the Coleman Report). Title I originally authorized more than a billion dollars, $6.7 billion in today's dollars, to upgrade the schools attended by children from low-income families. The program has continued to grow ever since, disposing of $12.7 billion in 2007. The link between Title I, aimed at poor children, and the school achievement of children who are below average in academic ability is indirect but strong. Poor children are disproportionately below average in academic ability. Whether the cause is poverty or the parents' genes (poor parents themselves tend to be below average in academic

ability) is immaterial. If Title I successfully raised academic performance in low-income neighborhoods, its effects would occur predominantly among children with low academic ability.

The supporters of Title I confidently expected to see progress, and
so formal evaluation of Title I was built into the legislation from the
beginning. Over the years, the evaluations have become progressively
more ambitious and more methodologically sophisticated. But while
the evaluations have improved, the story they tell has not changed.
Despite being conducted by people who wished the program well, no
evaluation of Title I from the 1970s onward has found credible
evidence of a significant positive impact on student achievement.
The plainest comparison of all is even worse than "no effect." The
Department of Education classifies schools as "high-poverty" schools
and "low-poverty" schools. The whole point of Title I is to narrow the
test score gap separating those two types of schools. A 2001 study by
the Department of Education revealed that the gap *widened* rather than
diminished from 1986, the earliest year such comparisons were made,
through 1999, the most recent year included in the study.

THE NO CHILD LEFT BEHIND ACT

Once an educational romantic has explained away Title I's lack of
effect, he is faced with a third reality test, the results of NCLB. If ever
an intervention were guaranteed to produce increases in test scores, it
is NCLB. It raised the stakes for educating students in the lower half
of the academic ability distribution to unprecedented levels, imposing
severe penalties on schools that failed to meet progress goals that
were set according to test scores. At the very least, the effects of
teaching to the test, which is occurring nationwide, should produce
increases in test scores even if the students are not learning more.

As in the case of the Long-Term Trend data, the results for reading and mathematics are different. At this point I switch from the Long-Term Trend data (which end in 2004) to the main administration of NAEP, so we can see the results through 2007. I again use students at the 25th percentile for the illustration. Readers can look at more detailed breakdowns from data available online.

Regarding the math test, we are faced with a complication: An administration of NAEP's math test wasn't on the schedule for 2002, when NCLB began. If we use the test given in 2000 as the baseline, then fourth-graders increased their mean score by seventeen points between 2000 and 2007 and eighth-graders increased their scores by nine points (score points, not percentile points). But if we use the 2003 test as the baseline, just one year after NCLB began, the increases were a modest six points and four points for fourth-graders and eighth-graders respectively. Whether you think NCLB is a success depends on which baseline you choose. There is no way to tell what happened to twelfth-graders in math—the 2005 test was too different from previous NAEP math tests to permit comparisons.

Can we say that NCLB is working for mathematics achievement? If the issue is statistical significance, the answer is unclear. I will wait for the psychometricians to complete the complex analyses that are necessary to decide. But the improvement cannot be large, after factoring out the gains that occurred between 2000 and 2002 before NCLB began.

Interpreting the reading scores is easy. NCLB was signed into law in January 2002. NAEP administered a reading test just a few months later, long before NCLB could have had an effect on test scores. Fourth-graders at the 25th percentile increased their mean score by three points between 2002 and 2007. The scores for eighth-graders *fell* by two points. Twelfth-graders were last tested in 2005. Their scores had also fallen since 2002, by one point. Such small changes up or down are meaningless. The effective change for students at the 25th percentile was zero, as were the changes among students at the 10th, 50th, 75th, and 90th percentiles. Judging from NAEP, NCLB has done nothing to raise reading skills despite the enormous effort that has been expended.

The Coleman Report documenting how little difference the quality of the school makes, the negative evaluations of Title I, the sparse results of NCLB—there are many reasons to accept the reality of limits. To continue to assert that major improvements are possible in the academic test performance of the lower half of the distribution through reform of the public schools is more than a triumph of hope over experience. It ignores experience altogether. It is educational romanticism.

ILLUSORY REASONS FOR THE ROMANTICISM

Why then do so many people still believe the contrary? Why was NCLB passed with a large bipartisan majority in Congress and with broad public support? Why will this chapter be greeted by all sorts of stories about teachers who took classes of failing students and had them reading Shakespeare in six months? There are four reasons that look good at first glance but cannot withstand scrutiny.

The first illusory reason is that some inner-city schools in some of the nation's largest cities are every bit as dreadful as people think. Accounts written by journalists, scholars, and teachers describe chaotic and sometimes violent classrooms, nonexistent standards, incompetent teachers, competent teachers who have given up, and lack of the most basic resources for teaching effectively, including textbooks. Rescuing children from such schools should be one of the top priorities of any educational reform, and doing so will produce improvements in their academic achievement.

But only a fraction of children attend such schools. Only 16 percent of all K–12 public school students go to schools that are located downtown in cities of 250,000 or larger. Twenty-three percent of the students in those cities are non-Hispanic whites, few of whom attend the worst inner-city schools. That leaves 12 percent of the nation's students, almost all of whom are black and Hispanic, in urban schools. Most of those schools are normal ones. What proportion of the 12 percent are going to the horrific schools? A quarter? A fifth? There is no precise answer, but any plausible estimate leaves us with much less than 10 percent of all K–12 students going to the worst schools, and the right proportion could easily be around 2 or 3 percent. Rescuing all of those children is something we must try to do, but even complete success would only tweak the national numbers.

The second illusory reason to think that there is a lot of room for improvement is that some of the national statistics artificially make the schools look terrible, especially the statistics showing that a large number of students are not performing at grade level. As I discussed earlier, interpreting those numbers is impossible without knowing how grade level is defined. We can translate this point into the problems of interpreting NAEP results. The 2007 round of tests found that 26 percent of all eighth-graders did not meet NAEP's standard for Basic reading achievement, the lowest of NAEP's achievement categories. It seems obvious that the schools could do a lot better. But before interpreting that number, one must know what level of linguistic ability is necessary to give a child a reasonable chance to score high enough to meet NAEP's definition of Basic in reading. Here is the description of the Basic level for eighth-graders:

Eighth-grade students performing at the *Basic* level should demonstrate a literal understanding of what they read and be able to make some interpretations. When reading text appropriate to eighth grade, they should be able to identify specific aspects of the text that reflect overall meaning, extend the ideas in the text by making simple inferences, recognize and relate interpretations and connections among ideas in the text to personal experience, and draw conclusions based on the text.

That sounds like the definition of someone who is not just functionally literate (able to read road signs, etc.) but literate by a more demanding definition that requires a fair amount of linguistic ability. But if, for example, a student needs linguistic ability at the 26th percentile to have a fifty-fifty chance of making a Basic reading score or better, then you have to expect that somewhere in the region of 26 percent of all students will fail to meet the Basic standard *even if the schools are successfully educating everyone up to their potential.* So what level of linguistic ability is in fact necessary to have a 50 percent chance of meeting the Basic standard? No one knows. As far as I have been able to determine, no one at the Department of Education has even asked anyone to look into it. But without knowing the answer to that question, there is no way of knowing whether 26 percent failing to meet the Basic standard is a sign of success or of failure.

The third illusory reason for romanticism about what schools can do is the nostalgic view that many people hold of American public schools in the good old days, when teachers brooked no nonsense and everyone learned their three R's. After all, just look at the McGuffey Readers that were standard textbooks in the nineteenth century, filled with difficult words and long literary selections. That's what we expected everyone to be able to read then, right?

Wrong. American schools have never been able to teach everyone how to read, write, and do arithmetic. The myth that they could has arisen because schools a hundred years ago did not have to educate many of the least able. Recall that about half of all adults in 1900 had not reached the eighth grade. To put it another way, only a small portion of those toward the bottom of linguistic ability would have been around to take a NAEP examination if it had been administered to eighth-graders in 1900. Let today's schools skim off the same part of the distribution, and they would show nearly 100 percent success in attaining the Basic standard in reading.

The final illusory reason for hope in the face of experience is the belief that private schools or variants such as charter schools can come to the rescue. I have long been an advocate of the privatization of American elementary and secondary education. I will be an advocate again in chapter 5, but not based on improvements in math and reading scores. Modest improvements in such scores, sometimes statistically significant, have been observed among students who get vouchers or go to charter schools and who would otherwise be consigned to the worst-of-the-worst schools in the inner city. But when the comparison is between a run-of-the-mill public school and a private school, math and reading test score differences have generally been minor or nonexistent. The real advantages of private or charter schools lie elsewhere—in the safe and orderly learning environments they offer their students (no small benefit), and in curricula that typically provide more substance in subjects like history, geography, literature, and civics than the curriculum offered by the typical public school. Private and charter schools often provide a supportive intellectual environment for hardworking students who, in public schools, are often subjected to peer pressures *not* to study—"nerd harassment," as it has been called. The accumulated data from assessments of Catholic private schools, voucher programs, and charter schools provides solid evidence that private and quasi-private education has many advantages over public education. But the evidence does not give reason to expect that private or charter schools produce substantially higher test scores in math and reading among low-ability students who would otherwise go to normal public schools.

No one wants to be education's Grinch, especially when we are talking about children who have gotten the short end of the stick through no fault of their own. The impulse to romanticism is overwhelming. But it has led us to do things to children who are below average in academic ability that are not in their best interests. The notion that we know how to make more than modest improvements in their math and reading performance has no factual basis. In assessing the state of American education, and what can be accomplished for the lower half of the distribution by any of the reforms proposed by either left or right, it is time to recognize that even the best schools under the best conditions cannot overcome the limits on achievement set by limits on academic ability.

This is not a counsel of despair. The implication is not to stop trying to help, but to stop doing harm. Educational romanticism has imposed immeasurable costs on children and their futures. It pursues unattainable egalitarian ideals of educational achievement (e.g., all children should perform at grade level) at the expense of attainable egalitarian ideals of personal dignity. We can do much better for children who are below average in academic ability, but only after we get a grip on reality.

Too Many People Are Going to College

I n the fall of 2005, more than 1.5 million students enrolled in America's four-year colleges or universities, a number equal to 50 percent of high school graduates that year. Almost all high school graduates need additional education. But a lot fewer than 1.5 million should be going to a four-year residential institution and trying to get a BA. One of the most damaging messages of educational romanticism has been that everyone should go to college.

This chapter discusses five topics. The first is a nuts-and-bolts issue: How smart do you have to be to cope with genuine college-level material? No more than 20 percent of students have that level of academic ability, and 10 percent is a more realistic estimate. The second topic is college's role in providing a liberal education. For all but a minority of students, that job should be done in elementary and secondary school. Next I turn to the ways in which colleges are becoming obsolete. Four years of residence on a college campus is seldom the best way to acquire the knowledge that most students want to acquire. The fourth topic is labeled "College isn't all it's cracked up to be." I make that case in terms of income, job satisfaction, and maturation. Finally, I turn to the divisive role that the college degree is acquiring in American society. By making a college degree something that everyone is supposed to want, we are punishing the majority of young people who do not get one.

The Intellectual Requirements for College-Level Work

To say that no more than 20 percent of all students have the academic ability to deal with college-level material seems to be false on its face, since the number of BAs awarded in 2005 amounted to 35 percent of all twenty-three-year-olds (I will use *BA* as shorthand for all bachelor's degrees and *college* as shorthand for four-year residential colleges or universities). It is also contradicted by studies of college readiness that say higher percentages of students, as many as 65 percent of high school graduates, are qualified for admission to a four-year college.

This brings us to a distinction that you should keep in mind throughout this chapter: the distinction between college-level instruction in the core disciplines of the arts and sciences, and the courses (and their level of difficulty) that are actually offered throughout much of the current American college system. With regard to this section of the chapter, I am asking how many high-school graduates can cope with college-level material in the core disciplines of the arts and sciences, not how many can survive four years at today's colleges and walk away with diplomas. If surviving to a diploma is the definition of "cope with college-level material," then almost anyone can do it if he shops for easy courses in an easy major at an easy college. But as soon as we focus on college-level material traditionally defined, the requirements become stringent.

For many years, the consensus intellectual benchmark for dealing with college-level material was an IQ of around 115, which demarcates the top 16 percent of the distribution. That was in fact the mean IQ of college graduates during the 1950s. It cannot be nearly that high today (not when 28 percent of adults twenty-five or older have a BA), but the intellectual requirements for coping with traditional college-level material have not changed. The best quantitative evidence for that statement comes from a study by the College Board that used a sample of forty-one colleges to assess the relationship of SAT scores to college readiness. The colleges in the sample ranged from state universities with student SAT means around the national average to highly selective elite schools (the most selective had a student SAT mean above 1250). In other words, they are all likely to have been colleges that actually teach college-level material as traditionally defined.

The College Board researchers defined college readiness as an SAT score that predicts a 65 percent probability or higher of getting a first-year college grade point average of 2.7 or higher—a B-minus average in an age of grade inflation, with no limitations on the courses that qualify. Even with this relaxed expectation, the benchmark scores were 590 for the SAT-Verbal, 610 for the SAT-Math, and 1180 or higher for the combined score (I will use the traditional labels, "Verbal" and "Math," for what are now officially called the Critical Reading and Mathematics sections of the SAT Reasoning Test). The benchmarks were not inflated by unusually high demands for the most selective colleges. The difference between the benchmarks of the unselective institutions and highly selective ones was only twenty-three points for the combined score. Nor were they inflated because many small colleges were part of the sample. The benchmarks were *lower* for schools with fewer than 3,000 students than for large state universities.

How many of America's seventeen-year-olds can meet the benchmarks? Three independent methods of calculating the answer to that question, described in the notes, lead to an estimate of 9 to 12 percent, with a realistic best-guess of about 10 percent.

So few can do well in real colleges because real college-level material is hard. This is obvious for engineering and most of the natural sciences, where students cannot get a degree unless they can handle the math. "Handle the math" means being able to pass courses in at least advanced calculus and statistics, a requirement that immediately makes the 10 percent estimate plausible. In the humanities and most of the social sciences, the difference between high school work and college-level work is fuzzier. It is possible for someone with average reading ability to sit through lectures and write answers in an examination book. But people with average reading ability do not understand much of the text in the assigned readings. They take away a mishmash of half-understood information and outright misunderstandings that probably leave them under the illusion they know something they do not.

Perhaps the best way to convey how tough it is to deal with genuine college-level material is to remind you what the books are like. Each of the following passages of about a hundred words is taken from texts commonly used for college survey courses. To quash the temptation to cherry-pick the most difficult text, I used the same page number for selecting each passage (page 400, chosen arbitrarily).

Western History. "The Protestant Reformation could not have occurred without the monumental crises of the medieval church during the 'exile' in Avignon, the Great Schism, the conciliar period, and the Renaissance papacy. For increasing numbers of people the medieval church had ceased also to provide a viable religious piety. There was a crisis in the traditional teaching and spiritual practice of the church among its many intellectuals and laity. Between the secular pretensions of the papacy and the dry teaching of Scholastic theologians, laity and clerics alike began to seek a more heartfelt, idealistic, and—often in the eyes of the pope—increasingly heretical religious piety." D. Kagan, S. Ozment, and F. M. Turner (1983). *The Western Heritage* (2nd ed.). New York: Macmillan.

Art. "Although the Humanists received with enthusiasm the new message from pagan antiquity, they nevertheless did not look upon themselves as pagans. It was possible for the fifteenth-century scholar Laurentius Valla to prove the forgery of the Donation of Constantine (an Early Medieval document purporting to record Constantine's bequest of the Roman empire to the Church) without feeling that he had compromised his Christian faith. The two great religious orders founded in the thirteenth century, the Dominicans and the Franciscans, were as dominant in setting the tone of fourteenth- and fifteenth-century Christian thought as they had been earlier, and they continued to be patrons of the arts." H. de la Croix & R. G. Tansey (1975). *Gardner's Art Through the Ages* (6th ed.). New York: Harcourt Brace Jovanovich.

Economics. "Suppose an industry like wine-grape growing requires a certain kind of soil and location (sunny hillsides, etc.). Such sites are limited in number. The annual output of wine can be increased to some extent by adding more labor and fertilizer to each acre of land and by bidding away some hill sites from other uses. But as we saw in chapter 2, the law of diminishing returns will begin to operate if variable factors of production, like labor and fertilizer, are added to fixed amounts of a factor like land. Why is that? Because each new variable addition of labor and fertilizer has a smaller proportion of land to work with." P. A. Samuelson & W. D. Nordhaus (1985). *Economics* (12th ed.). New York: McGraw-Hill.

Psychology. "An exciting feature of artificial neural networks is their capacity to learn from experience, as some interconnections strengthen and others weaken. Their learning, together with their capacity for parallel processing, enables neural network computers to pick up how to navigate, play soccer, mimic others' expressions, and recognize particular shapes, sounds, and smells—tasks that conventional computers find extremely difficult. A striking example: Thomas Landauer and his colleagues applied principles of computer neural networking to 'read' a previous edition of this textbook. As their 'Latent Semantic Analysis' program read the entire book, it associated all the individual words with one another." D. G. Myers (2004). *Psychology* (7th ed.). New York: Worth Publishers.

Philosophy. "The most prominent philosophical outcome of these several converging strands of postmodern thought has been a many-sided critical attack on the central Western philosophical tradition from Platonism onward. The whole project of that tradition to grasp and articulate a foundational Reality has been criticized as a futile exercise in linguistic game playing, a sustained but doomed effort to move beyond elaborate fictions of its own creation. More pointedly, such a project has been condemned as inherently alienating and oppressively hierarchical —an intellectually imperious procedure that has produced an existential and cultural impoverishment, and that has led ultimately to the technocratic domination of nature and the social-political domination of others." R. Tarnas (1991). *The Passion of the Western Mind: Understanding the Ideas That Have Shaped Our World View.* New York: Ballantine Books.

English Literature: "If a man chooses to call every composition a poem which is rhyme, or measure, or both, I must leave his opinion uncontroverted. The distinction is at least competent to characterize the writer's intention. If it were subjoined that the whole is likewise entertaining or affecting as a tale or as a series of interesting reflections, I of course admit this as another fit ingredient of a poem and an additional merit. But if the definition sought for be that of a *legitimate* poem, I answer it must be one the parts of which mutually support and explain each other." Samuel Taylor Coleridge, "Biographica Literaria." In M. H. Abrams et al. (eds.), *The Norton Anthology of English Literature* (4th ed., Vol. 2, 1979). New York: W. W. Norton & Co.

On any random page of textbooks for introductory courses in the core college disciplines, that's the kind of prose that a freshman must be prepared to read and understand. It's not easy. The sentences in the passages average twenty-six words (by way of comparison, the length of the average sentence in a well-regarded high school history textbook is thirteen). Long sentences demand a high degree of focus even if the syntax and vocabulary are simple. But the syntax in the passages I just quoted actually ranges from demanding to tortuous, involving intertwined independent and dependent clauses and frequent interpolations of material. Then the reader has to figure out what the words mean, and the barriers are many. The passages are studded with unexplained references that impede understanding if the reader is unfamiliar with them (*Avignon, diminishing returns, Dominicans, Early Medieval, Franciscans, Great Schism, Humanists, parallel processing, Platonism, Reformation, Renaissance, Scholastics*). Then there are the words that most students use in ordinary conversation, but are being used in the text to convey a less familiar, sometimes downright obscure meaning ("... *admit* this as another *fit* ingredient ...," "... is *affecting* as a tale ...," "... by *bidding* away some hill sites ...," "... *fixed* amounts ...," "... the distinction is at least *competent* to characterize ...," "... he had *compromised* his Christian faith ...," "... a futile *exercise*," "... elaborate *fictions* of its own creation," "... rhyme, or *measure*, or both ...," "... religious *orders*," "... the whole *project* of that tradition"). Finally, there is the relentless use of words that not many high-school seniors know. Excluding the specialized vocabulary and historical references, these short passages contain twelve words that are not among the 20,000 most frequently used English words: *alienating, clerics, conciliar, foundational, heretical, imperious, impoverishment, interconnections, pretensions, subjoined, technocratic,* and *uncontroverted.* Nor should one bet that more than a minority of high-school seniors know *antiquity, articulate, characterize, converging, existential, hierarchical, inherently, laity, latent, monumental, neural, pagan, papacy, patrons, piety, pointedly, semantic,* and *viable.*

All of these difficulties arise in passages totaling not much more than the length of a single page in a typical college textbook. The intellectual demands of traditional college-level material in the social sciences and humanities cannot be described as concretely as they can for engineering, mathematics, and the sciences, but they are as severe in their own way.

We can put a range of numbers on part of the simple truth that too many people are going to college. Purely on the basis of intellectual qualifications, the number of freshmen in four-year institutions is roughly 1.8 times the appropriate number if we use the top 20 percent in academic ability as the right cutoff and 2.1 times the appropriate number if 15 percent is the right cutoff. For sterner souls who agree I have just presented evidence that 10 percent is the right cutoff, then 3.3 times the appropriate number are enrolling. Whatever cutoff you prefer, they are all underestimates—none of them includes another set of students who meet the intellectual cutoff but do not really want what college is designed to provide. And that brings us to two vexed questions:

Who Should Acquire a Liberal Education? When?

To ask whether too many people are going to college requires us to think about the importance and nature of a liberal education. "Universities are not intended to teach the knowledge required to fit men for some special mode of gaining their livelihood," John Stuart Mill told students at the University of St Andrews in 1867. "Their object is not to make skilful lawyers, or physicians, or engineers, but capable and cultivated human beings." If this is true (and I agree that it is), why say that too many people are going to college? Surely a mass democracy should encourage as many people as possible to become "capable and cultivated human beings" in Mill's sense. We should not restrict the availability of a liberal education to a rarefied intellectual elite. More people should be going to college, not fewer.

E. D. Hirsch's Core Knowledge as the Skeleton of a Liberal Education

Yes and no. More people should be getting the basics of a liberal education. But for most students, the places to provide those basics are elementary and middle school. E. D. Hirsch Jr. is the indispensable thinker on this topic, beginning with his 1987 book *Cultural Literacy: What Every American Needs to Know.* Part of his argument involves the importance of a body of core knowledge in fostering reading speed and comprehension, an important pedagogical finding that I discuss in the notes to this chapter. With regard to a liberal education, Hirsch makes three points that are germane here:

Full participation in any culture requires familiarity with a body of core knowledge. To live in the United States and not recognize Teddy Roosevelt, Prohibition, Minutemen, Huckleberry Finn, Wall Street, smoke-filled room, or Gettysburg is like trying to read without knowing some of the ten thousand most commonly used words in the language. It signifies a degree of cultural illiteracy about America. But the core knowledge transcends one's own country. Not to recognize Falstaff, Apollo, Sistine Chapel, Inquisition, Twenty-third Psalm, or Mozart signifies cultural illiteracy about the West. Not to recognize solar system, Big Bang, natural selection, relativity, or periodic table is to be scientifically illiterate. Not to recognize Mediterranean, Vienna, Yangtze River, Mount Everest, or Mecca is to be geographically illiterate.

This core knowledge is an important part of the glue that holds the culture together. All American children, of whatever ethnic heritage, and whether their families came here three hundred years ago or three months ago, need to learn about the Pilgrims, Valley Forge, Duke Ellington, Apollo 11, Susan B. Anthony, George C. Marshall, and the Freedom Riders. All students need to learn the iconic stories. For a society of immigrants such as ours, the core knowledge is our shared identity that makes us Americans together rather than hyphenated Americans.

K–8 are the right years to teach the core knowledge, and the effort should get off to a running start in elementary school. Starting early is partly a matter of necessity: There's a lot to learn, and it takes time. But another reason is that small children enjoy learning myths and fables, showing off names and dates they have memorized, and hearing about great historical figures and exciting deeds. The educational establishment sees this kind of curriculum as one that forces children to memorize boring facts. That conventional wisdom is wrong on every count. The facts can be fascinating (if taught right); a lot more than memorization is entailed; yet memorizing things is an indispensable part of education, too; and memorizing is something that children do much, much better than adults. The core knowledge is suited to ways that young children naturally learn and enjoy learning. Not all children will be able to do the reading with the same level of comprehension, but the fact-based nature of the core knowledge actually works to the benefit of low-ability students—remembering facts is much easier than making inferences and deductions. The core knowledge curriculum lends itself to adaptation for students across a wide range of academic ability.

In the twenty years since *Cultural Literacy* was published, Hirsch and his colleagues have developed and refined his original formulation into an inventory of more than six thousand items that approximate the core knowledge broadly shared by literate Americans. Hirsch's Core Knowledge Foundation has also developed a detailed, grade-by-grade curriculum for K–8, complete with lists of books and other teaching materials.

The table on page 79 illustrates the Core Knowledge curriculum with the topics taught in third grade. For purposes of comparison, I have also put in the third-grade curriculum as described on the website of a well-regarded public school system—specifically, the public schools of Frederick County, Maryland, that my two younger children attended. I have omitted topics involving the mechanics of reading, writing, and arithmetic. Both curricula cover roughly the same material. The discrepancy comes in everything else, as the table shows.

The first curriculum presented in the table is the kind of knowledge that, accumulated over the nine years from kindergarten through eighth grade, will make children culturally literate. In effect, it also gives them the skeleton of a liberal education. The second curriculum is representative of a typical progressive school. The problem is not that the progressive curriculum takes too little effort. Frederick County teachers work hard and the children are given lots of homework—arguably, too much homework for children their age. The problem is not the effort, but the anemic content. Lots of process, lots of experiential learning, lots of politically fashionable blather. Not much meat and potatoes.

The Core Knowledge approach need not stop with eighth grade. High school is a good place for survey courses in the humanities, social sciences, and sciences taught at a level below the demands of a college course and accessible to most students in the upper two-thirds of the distribution of academic ability. Some students will not want to take these courses, and it can be counterproductive to require them to do so—more on that in chapter 5—but high school can put

Two Third-Grade Curricula

R E A D I N G

The Core Knowledge Curriculum.

Poetry by Lewis Carroll, Nikki Giovanni, Langston Hughes, Eve Merriam, & Ogden Nash.

Read or are read *Alice in Wonderland,* tales from *The Arabian Nights,* "The Little Match Girl," "William Tell," selections from *Wind in the Willows,* Norse myths, Greek & Roman myths, & folktales from around the world.

Frederick County Public Schools

Comprehension. How to identify grade-appropriate text, how to identify ideas & information while reading. "Read a variety of literature such as folktales, fairytales, poetry, newspapers, magazines, & Internet Web sites."

S O C I A L   S T U D I E S

The Core Knowledge Curriculum

World Geography. The Mediterranean region, Canada, use of an atlas, measuring distance on a map, important world rivers & associated terms (e.g., source, tributary, delta, strait).

World History. Ancient Rome (Romulus & Remus, adaptation of Greek gods, Julius Caesar, life in the Roman Empire, Pompeii, Constantine & Christianity, rise of Byzantium, the decline & fall of Rome). The Vikings (culture, their exploration of North America).

American History. The earliest Americans (tribes of the Southwest & Eastern Woodlands). Early exploration of North America (Spanish exploration of the Southeast & Southwest, search for the Northwest Passage). Settlement of the Thirteen Colonies, with extended treatment of New York, Pennsylvania, Virginia, Massachusetts, & development of the slave trade.

Frederick County Public Schools

Peoples of the Nation & World. No specific peoples. Sample of curricula: "Describe the benefits of a multicultural setting."

History. No specific period or place. Sample of curricula: "Explain how people lived in the past by using a variety of primary & secondary sources."

Geography. No specific region or geographic features. Sample of curricula: "Locate & describe places using geographic tools."

Economics. No specific economic system. Sample of curricula: "Explain the decision-making process used to make an economic choice."

Political Science. Emphasis on democratic principles. Sample of curricula: "Explain the roles of individuals & groups in creating rules & laws."

The Core Knowledge Curriculum

Introduction to the Classification of Animals. Warm-blooded & cold-blooded. Characteristics & examples of vertebrates, invertebrates, amphibians, reptiles, birds, mammals.

Human Body. Muscular, skeletal, & nervous systems; how the eye & ear work.

Light & Optics. Use a prism to learn about the spectrum. Use different types of lenses & learn associated terms (e.g., transparent, opaque).

Sound. Causes of sound & differences in pitch, transmission of sound through substances, physiology of the human voice.

Ecology. Ecosystems, the food chain, effects of human activity.

Astronomy. Galaxies, planetary motion & its effects on seasons, gravity, stars, eclipses, space exploration.

Science Biographies (e.g., Copernicus, Alexander Graham Bell, John Muir).

Frederick County Public Schools

Life Science: Populations Unit. Sample of curricula: "Observe & diagram the feeding interactions among land & aquatic populations of plants, plant-eaters, & animal-eaters."

Earth Science: Water Planet Unit. Sample of curricula: "Explain that making choices about the environment has consequences of varying degrees."

Physical Science: Subsystems & Variables Unit. Sample of curricula: "Explain 'subsystem' as it refers to a system that is part of another system."

The Core Knowledge Curriculum

Elements of Music. Recognition of harmony, themes & variations. Musical notation.

Listening & Understanding. The orchestra, focusing on bass & woodwind instruments, illustrated with works by Rossini, Beethoven, Copland, Gilbert & Sullivan, Rimsky-Korsakov & Wagner.

Frederick County Public Schools

Music class. No description of curriculum.

The Core Knowledge Curriculum

Elements of Art. The use of light & shadow illustrated with works by Vermeer & others. Different ways to create the illusion of depth, illustrated with works by Bruegel & others. Combining patterns, balance & symmetry to create designs, illustrated by Matisse cutouts, American quilts, Navajo weavings, & sandpainting. Use of design to tell a story, illustrated with works by Dali & others.

American Indian Art

Art of Ancient Rome & Byzantine Civilization

Frederick County Public Schools

Art class. No description of curriculum.

considerable flesh on the liberal education skeleton for students who are still interested.

In summary: Saying "too many people are going to college" is not the same as saying that the average student does not need to know about history, science, and great works of art, music, and literature. They do need to know—and to know more than they are currently learning. So let's teach it to them, but let's not wait for college to do it.

LIBERAL EDUCATION IN COLLEGE

Liberal education in college means taking on the tough stuff. A high-school graduate who has acquired Hirsch's core knowledge will know, for example, that John Stuart Mill was an important nineteenth-century English philosopher who was associated with something called Utilitarianism and wrote a famous book called *On Liberty*. But learning philosophy in college, which is an essential component of a liberal education, means that the student has to be able to read and understand the actual text of *On Liberty*. That brings us back to the limits set by the nature of college-level material. Here is the first sentence of *On Liberty:* "The subject of this essay is not the so-called liberty of the will, so unfortunately opposed to the mis-named doctrine of philosophical necessity; but civil, or social liberty: the nature and limits of the power which can be legitimately exercised by society over the individual." I will not burden you with *On Liberty*'s last sentence. It is 126 words long. And Mill is one of the more accessible philosophers, and *On Liberty* is one of Mill's more accessible works. It would be nice if everyone could acquire a fully formed liberal education, but they cannot. We are once again looking at the 20 percent tops, and probably closer to 10 percent, who have the level of academic ability necessary to cope with the stuff of a liberal education at the college level.

Should all of those who *do* have the academic ability to absorb a college-level liberal education get one? It depends. Suppose we have before us a young woman who is in the 98th percentile of academic ability and wants to become a lawyer and eventually run for political office. To me, it seems essential that she spend her undergraduate years getting a rigorous liberal education. I will make this case in detail in the next chapter. The short version is that, apart from a liberal education's value to her, the nation will benefit. Everything she does as an attorney or as an elected official should be informed by the kind of wisdom that a rigorous liberal education can encourage. It is appropriate to push her into that kind of undergraduate program.

But the only reason we can get away with pushing her is that the odds are high that she will enjoy it. The odds are high because she is good at this sort of thing—it's no problem for her to read *On Liberty* or *Paradise Lost*. It's no problem for her to come up with an interesting perspective on what she's read and weave it into a term paper. And because she's good at it, she is also likely to enjoy it. It is one of Aristotle's central themes in his discussion of human happiness, a theme that John Rawls later distilled into what he called the Aristotelian Principle: "Other things equal, human beings enjoy the exercise of their realized capacities (their innate or trained abilities), and this enjoyment increases the more the capacity is realized, or the greater its complexity." And so it comes to pass that those who take the hardest majors and who enroll in courses that look most like an old-fashioned liberal education are concentrated among the students in the top percentiles of academic ability. Getting a liberal education consists of dealing with complex intellectual material day after day, and dealing with complex intellectual material is what students in the top few percentiles are really good at, in the same way that other people are really good at cooking or making pottery. For these students, doing it well is fun.

Every percentile down the ability ladder—and this applies to all abilities, not just academic—the probability that a person will enjoy the hardest aspects of an activity goes down as well. Students at the 80th percentile of academic ability are still smart kids, but the odds that they will respond to a course that assigns Mill or Milton are considerably lower than the odds that a student in the top few percentiles will respond. Virtue has nothing to do it. Maturity has nothing to do with it. Appreciation of the value of a liberal education has nothing to do with it. The probability that a student will enjoy *Paradise Lost* goes down as his linguistic ability goes down, but so does the probability that he works on double acrostic puzzles in his spare time or plays online Scrabble hour after hour, and for the identical reason. The lower down the linguistic ladder he is, the less fun such activities are.

And so we return to the question: Should all of those who have the academic ability to absorb a college-level liberal education get one? If our young woman is at the 80th percentile of linguistic ability, should she be pushed to do so? She has enough intellectual capacity, if she puts her mind to it and works exceptionally hard.

The answer is no. If she wants to, fine. But she probably won't, and there's no way to force her. Try to force her (for example, by setting up a demanding core curriculum), and she will transfer to another school, because she is in college for vocational training. She wants to write computer code. Start a business. Get a job in television. She uses college to take vocational courses that pertain to her career interests. A large proportion of people who are theoretically able to absorb a liberal education have no interest in doing so.

And reasonably so. Seen dispassionately, getting a traditional liberal education over four years is an odd way to enjoy spending one's time. Not many people enjoy reading for hour after hour, day after day, no matter what the material may be. To enjoy reading *On Liberty* and its ilk—and if you're going to absorb such material, you must in some sense enjoy the process—is downright peculiar. To be willing to spend many more hours writing papers and answers to exam questions about that material approaches masochism.

We should look at the kind of work that goes into acquiring a liberal education at the college level in the same way that we look at the grueling apprenticeship that goes into becoming a master chef: something that understandably attracts only a limited number of people. Most students at today's colleges choose not to take the courses that go into a liberal education because the capabilities they want to develop lie elsewhere. These students are not lazy, any more than students who don't want to spend hours learning how to chop carrots into a perfect eighth-inch dice are lazy. A liberal education just doesn't make sense for them.

Colleges do their best to avoid admitting this. Because the BA is still supposed to signify that its possessor has acquired a liberal education, almost every college pays lip service to that tradition by stipulating that students must take a certain number of classes outside their major and that those classes must be distributed among the disciplines that traditionally went into a liberal education. Students then examine the course catalog and select the courses that will check off the humanities box, the social sciences box, and the natural sciences box.

They are unlikely to have much guidance in this task. Few parents even try to guide their children's choice of college courses, and still fewer succeed. Faculty advice is usually limited to telling students what they will need to fulfill their major requirements or what courses a law school or medical school wants to see on an application. Otherwise, college students are left to make their own choices. They tend to make two kinds of mistakes.

Some students take the distribution requirements seriously, but don't want to take the broad survey courses in history, literature, philosophy, the sciences, and the arts that would in fact give them a decent liberal education. They see course titles such as "European History from the Renaissance to World War I" or "The Epic Poem from Homer to Milton" and, remembering that they studied European history in eleventh grade and read the *Odyssey* in ninth grade, think to themselves that they already know that stuff. So they fulfill the literature requirement with a course on twentieth-century French drama instead of the epic poem and fulfill the history requirement with a course on medieval Japan instead of taking the survey course on European history. Their enthusiasm for trying something new is understandable (I am reporting the logic behind my own odd course choices when I was an undergraduate), but they leave students with gaping holes in their education. The European history of the high-school course is nothing like the European history of a good college course; reading the *Odyssey* in ninth grade is nothing like reading the *Odyssey* in a good college course. Distribution requirements that do not require the survey courses do not produce many undergraduates who acquire a liberal education even among those who are eager to push themselves.

Other students see the distribution requirements as a distraction from their real interests and something to be gotten out of the way with the least work and the most fun. If they can choose between checking off the humanities box by taking "The Epic Poem from Homer to Milton" or "The Epic Film from *Ben Hur* to *Lord of the Rings,*" they opt for the latter. I made up that one, but here are samples of actual courses that fulfilled humanities and literature requirements at major schools as of 2004: "History of Comic Book Art" (Indiana University), "History and Philosophy of Dress" (Texas Tech University), "Love and Money" (Bryn Mawr), "Survey of World Cinema" (University of Illinois), "Ghosts, Demons, and Monsters" (Dartmouth), "Rock Music from 1970 to the Present" (University of Illinois), "American Popular Culture and Folklife" (Penn State University). At Duke, you could fulfill a social science requirement with "Campus Culture and Drinking."

Hardly any colleges require the demanding survey courses that are the foundation of a liberal education. The course examples I just listed were drawn from a study of fifty colleges, including the most prestigious ones. The study inventoried their requirements for course work in literature, composition, foreign language, American government or history, economics, mathematics, and the natural sciences. Remedial writing and mathematics courses did not count, nor did a distribution requirement that could be met by a course that focused on a narrow era or specialty. Out of the fifty institutions, none had core course requirements for all seven categories. Baylor did the best, with a requirement for six of them. Thirty-five of the fifty institutions required core courses in three categories or fewer. The twelve colleges that required just two included Harvard, Princeton, and Yale. The ten that required only one included Berkeley, Cornell, and Smith. Two colleges, Brown and Vassar, required none. Distribution requirements *could* serve the broadening function of a liberal education, but they hardly ever do.

It is appropriate that the meaning of the BA be intertwined with the concept of a liberal education. That's why four years makes sense—it takes that long to get a solid grounding in the many elements of a liberal education. That's why a degree makes sense instead of some other way of more directly measuring what a student has learned: If undergraduate education consists of a set of core courses that everyone has to take, then it is possible to attach meaning to a piece of paper with "Bachelor of Arts" on it. But colleges are no longer in the business of imparting a liberal education. The educational goals of most students now in college have nothing to do with such a thing. In a reasonable world, these students would have better options than going from high school to college.

For Learning How to Make a Living, the Four-Year Brick-and-Mortar Residential College Is Increasingly Obsolete

We now go from one extreme to the other, from the ideal of liberal education to the utilitarian process of acquiring the knowledge that most students go to college to acquire—practical and vocational. The question here is not whether the traditional four-year residential college is fun or valuable as a place to grow up, but when it makes sense as a place to learn how to make a living. The answer is: in a sensible world, hardly ever.

Four years is almost always too long. Start with the time it takes—four years. Assuming a semester system with four courses per semester, four years of class work means thirty-two semester-long courses. The occupations for which "knowing enough" requires thirty-two courses are exceedingly rare. For some professions—medicine and law are the obvious examples—a rationale for four years of course work can be concocted (combining pre-med and pre-law undergraduate courses with three years of medical school and law school), but for every other occupation, the body of knowledge taught in classrooms can be learned more quickly. Even PhDs don't require four years of coursework. The PhD is supposed to signify expertise, but that expertise comes from burrowing deep into a specialty, not from dozens of courses.

Those are the jobs with the most stringent academic requirements. For the student who wants to become a good hotel manager, software designer, accountant, hospital administrator, farmer, high-school teacher, social worker, journalist, optometrist, interior designer, or football coach, four years of class work is ridiculous. Actually becoming good in those occupations will take longer than four years, but most of the competence is acquired on the job. The two-year community college and online courses offer more flexible options for tailoring course work to the real needs of the job.

A brick-and-mortar campus is increasingly obsolete. The physical infrastructure of the college used to make sense for three reasons. First, a good library was essential to higher learning, and only a college faculty and student body provided the economies of scale that made good libraries affordable. Second, scholarship flourishes through colleagueships, and the college campus made it possible to put scholars in physical proximity to each other. Third, the best teaching requires interaction between teachers and students, and physical proximity was the only way to get it. All three rationales for the brick-and-mortar campus are fading fast.

The rationale for a physical library is within a few years of extinction. Even now, the Internet provides access, for a price, to all the world's significant technical journals. The books are about to follow. Google is scanning the entire text of every book in the libraries of Harvard, Princeton, Stanford, Oxford, the New York Public Library, the Bavarian State Library, Ghent University Library, Keio Library (Tokyo), the National University of Catalonia, University of Lausanne, University of Mysore, and an expanding list of others. Collectively, this project will encompass close to the sum total of human knowledge. It will be completely searchable. Everything out of copyright will be free. Everything still under copyright will be accessible for a fee. Libraries will still be a selling point for colleges, but as a place for students to study in pleasant surroundings—an amenity in the same way that an attractive student union is an amenity. Colleges and universities will not *need* to exist because they provide libraries.

The rationale for colleges based on colleagueships has eroded. Until a few decades ago, physical proximity was important because correspondence and phone calls just weren't as good. As e-mail began to spread in universities during the 1980s, physical proximity became less important. As the capacity of the Internet expanded in the 1990s, other mechanisms made those interactions richer. Now, regular e-mails from professional groups inform scholars of the latest publications in their field of interest. Specialized chat groups enable scholars to bounce new ideas off other people working on the same problems. Drafts are exchanged effortlessly and comments attached electronically. Whether physical proximity still has any advantages depends mostly on the personality of the scholar. Some people like being around other people during the workday and prefer face-to-face conversations to e-mails. For those who don't, the value of being on a college campus instead of on a mountaintop in Montana is nil. Their electronic access to other scholars is incomparably greater than any scholar enjoyed even within the world's premier universities before the advent of the Internet. Like the library, face-to-face colleagueships will be an amenity that colleges continue to provide. But colleges and universities will not *need* to exist because they provide a community of scholars.

The third rationale for the brick-and-mortar college is that it brings teachers together with students. Working against that rationale is the explosion in the breadth and realism of what is known as *distance learning*. The idea of distance learning is surprisingly old—Isaac Pitman was teaching his shorthand system to British students through the postal service in the 1840s, and the University of London began offering degrees for correspondence students in 1858—but the technology of distance learning changed little for the next century. The advent of inexpensive videocassettes in the 1980s opened up a way for students to hear and see lectures without being in the classroom. By the early 1990s, it was possible to buy college-level courses on audio- or videotape, taught by first-rate teaching professors, on a wide range of topics, for a few hundred dollars. But without easy interaction between teacher and student, distance learning remained a poor second-best to a good college seminar.

Once again, the Internet is revolutionizing everything. As personal computers acquired the processing power to show high-definition video and the storage capacity to handle big video files, the possibilities for distance learning expanded by orders of magnitude. We are now watching the early expression of those possibilities: podcasts and streaming videos in real time of professors' lectures, online discussions among students scattered around the country, online interaction between students and professors, online exams, and tutorials augmented by computer-aided instruction software.

Even today, the quality of student-teacher interactions in a virtual classroom competes with the interactions in a brick-and-mortar classroom. But the technology is still in its early stages of development and the rate of improvement is breathtaking. Compare video games such as Myst and Sim City in the 1990s to their descendants today; the Walkman you used in the 1990s to the iPod you use today; the cell phone you used in the 1990s to the BlackBerry or iPhone you use today. Whatever technical limitations might lead you to say, "Yes, but it's still not the same as being there in the classroom," are probably within a few years of being outdated.

College Isn't All It's Cracked Up to Be

College looms so large in the thinking of both parents and students because it is seen as the open sesame to a good job. It has also become commonly accepted that four years on a college campus is a desirable way for young people to make the transition from adolescence to adulthood. On examination, neither reason is as persuasive as it first appears.

THE WAGE PREMIUM OF THE BA

When high-school graduates think that obtaining a BA will help them get a higher-paying job, they are only narrowly correct. Economists have established beyond doubt that people with BAs earn more on average than people without them. But why does the BA produce that result? For whom does the BA produce that result?

For some jobs, the economic premium for a degree is produced by the actual education that has gone into getting the degree. Lawyers, physicians, and engineers can earn their high incomes only by deploying knowledge and skills that take years to acquire, and degrees in law, medicine, and engineering still signify competence in those knowledges and skills. But for many other jobs, the economic premium for the BA is created by a brutal fact of life about the American job market: Employers do not even interview applicants who do not hold a BA. Even more brutal, the advantage conferred by the BA often has nothing to do with content of the education. Employers do not value what the student learned, just that the student has a degree.

Employers value the BA because it is a no-cost (for them) screening device for academic ability and perseverance. The more people who go to college, the more sense it makes for employers to require a BA. When only a small percentage of people got college degrees, employers who required a BA would have been shutting themselves off from access to most of the talent. With more than a third of twenty-three-year-olds now getting a BA, many employers can reasonably limit their hiring pool to college graduates because bright and ambitious high-school graduates who can go to college usually do go to college. An employer can believe that exceptions exist but rationally choose not to expend time and money to identify them. Knowing this, large numbers of students are in college to buy their admission ticket—the BA.

But while it is true that the average person with a BA makes more than the average person without a BA, getting a BA is still going to be the wrong economic decision for many high-school graduates. Wages within occupations form a distribution. Young people with okay-but-not-great academic ability who are thinking about whether to go after a BA need to consider the competition they will face after they graduate. Let me put these calculations in terms of a specific example, a young man who has just graduated from high school and is trying to decide whether to become an electrician or go to college and major in business, hoping to become a white-collar manager. He is at the 70th percentile in linguistic ability and logical-mathematical ability—someone who shouldn't go to college by my standards, but who can, in today's world, easily find a college that will give him a degree. He is exactly average in interpersonal and intrapersonal ability. He is at the 95th percentile in the small-motor skills and spatial abilities that are helpful in being a good electrician.

He begins by looking up the average income of electricians and managers on the Bureau of Labor Statistics website, and finds that the mean annual income for electricians in 2005 was $45,630, only about half of the $88,450 mean for management occupations. It looks as if getting a BA will buy him a huge wage premium. Should he try to get the BA on economic grounds?

To make his decision correctly, our young man must start by throwing out the averages. He has the ability to become an excellent electrician and can reasonably expect to be near the top of the electricians' income distribution. He does not have it in him to be an excellent manager, because he is only average in interpersonal and intrapersonal ability and only modestly above average in academic ability, all of which are important for becoming a good manager, while his competitors for those slots will include many who are high in all of those abilities. Realistically, he should be looking at the incomes toward the bottom of the distribution of managers. With that in mind, he goes back to the Bureau of Labor Statistics website and discovers that an electrician at the 90th percentile of electricians' incomes made

$70,480 in 2005, almost twice the income of a manager at the 10th percentile of managers' incomes ($37,800). Even if our young man successfully completes college and gets a BA (which is far from certain), he is likely to make less money than if he becomes an electrician.

Then there is job security to consider. A good way to make sure you always can find work is to be among the best at what you do. It also helps to have a job that does not require you to compete with people around the globe. When corporations downsize, they lay off mediocre managers before they lay off top electricians. When the economy gets soft, top electricians can find work when mediocre managers cannot. Low-level management jobs can often be outsourced to India, whereas electricians' jobs cannot.

What I have said of electricians is true throughout the American job market. The income for the top people in a wide variety of occupations that do not require a college degree is higher than the average income for many occupations that require a BA. Furthermore, the range and number of such jobs is expanding rapidly. The need for assembly-line workers in factories (one of the most boring jobs ever invented) is falling, but the demand for skilled technicians of every kind—in health care, information technology, transportation networks, and every other industry that relies on high-tech equipment—is expanding. The service sector includes many low-skill, low-paying jobs, but it also includes growing numbers of specialized jobs that pay well (for example, in health care and the entertainment and leisure industries). Construction offers an array of high-paying jobs for people who are good at what they do. It's not just skilled labor in the standard construction trades that is in high demand. The increase in wealth in American society has increased the demand for all sorts of craftsmanship. Today's high-end homes and office buildings may entail the work of specialized skills in stonework, masonry, glazing, painting, cabinetmaking, machining, landscaping, and a dozen other crafts. The increase in wealth is also driving an increased demand for the custom-made and the exquisitely wrought, meaning demand for artisans in everything from pottery to jewelry to metalworking. There has never been a time in history when people with skills not taught in college have been in so much demand at such high pay as today, nor a time when the range of such jobs has been so wide. In today's America, finding a first-rate lawyer or physician is easy. Finding first-rate skilled labor is hard.

INTRINSIC REWARDS

The topic is no longer money but job satisfaction—intrinsic rewards. We return to our high-school graduate trying to decide between going to college and becoming an electrician. He knows that he enjoys working with his hands and likes the idea of not being stuck in the same place all day, but he also likes the idea of being a manager sitting behind a desk in a big office, telling people what to do and getting the status that goes with it.

However, he should face facts that he is unlikely to know on his own, but that a guidance counselor could help him face. His chances of getting the big office and the status are slim. He is more likely to remain in a cubicle, under the thumb of the boss in the big office. He is unlikely to have a job in which he produces something tangible during the course of the day.

If he becomes a top electrician instead, he will have an expertise that he exercises at a high level. At the end of a workday, he will often be able to see that his work made a difference in the lives of people whose problems he has solved. He will not be confined to a cubicle and, after his apprenticeship, will be his own supervisor in the field. Top electricians often become independent contractors who have no boss at all.

The intrinsic rewards of being a top manager can be just as great as those of a top electrician (though I would not claim they are greater), but the intrinsic rewards of being a mediocre manager are not. Even as people in white-collar jobs lament the soullessness of their work, the intrinsic rewards of exercising technical skills remain undiminished.

Finally, there is an overarching consideration so important it is hard to express adequately: the satisfaction of being good at what one does for a living (and knowing it), compared to the melancholy of being mediocre at what one does for a living (and knowing it). This is another truth about living a human life that a seventeen-year-old might not yet understand on his own, but that a guidance counselor can bring to his attention.

Guidance counselors and parents who automatically encourage young people to go to college straight out of high school regardless of their skills and interests are being thoughtless about the best interests of young people in their charge. Even for students who have the academic ability to succeed in college, going directly to college may be a bad way for them to discover who they are and how they should make a living.

College as a Place to Mature

In addition to deciding what they want to do for a living when they grow up, eighteen-year-old high-school graduates have a lot of growing up to do. Where is the best place for them to do it?

It is possible to envision a college that would be a terrific place to grow up. In this idealized college, young people are living away from home, responsible for the first time for making decisions about personal behavior. Students cannot count on the Dean of Students to make allowances for childish mistakes, and must learn to think ahead and weigh the potential consequences of behavior, just as in adult life. The college curriculum demands the students' most strenuous efforts, so that students who succeed in getting degrees must necessarily have learned how to allocate their time, set priorities, and discipline themselves. They also have learned what it is like to work hard over a long period of time.

In this idealized college, students must behave with their professors much as they will have to behave with employers in adult life. They are not on an equal footing with their professors, but in a student-teacher relationship that bears some similarities to the subordinate-supervisor relationships that they will have to negotiate when they get jobs in the real world. Students must also accept that the point is not whether they try hard, but whether they get the job done. If they don't get the job done, they are flunked with as little ceremony as they will be fired in adult life.

I have focused on the life-is-real-and-life-is-earnest functions of the college environment, but they need not dominate day-to-day life. My idealized college is a pleasant place to spend four years, with a sylvan campus, an engaged faculty, comfortable dorms, and parties on the weekends. But it provides a bridge between childhood and adulthood, giving adolescents practice in meeting the kinds of responsibilities that are part of being an adult.

I cannot say, confidently that my idealized college environment has ever existed, but, without doubt, it bears no resemblance to the environment of today's typical college. The light workload alone can make college a joke. Students have a wide choice of easy courses in easy majors, and many students don't do the work that even these require. The most recent (2007) survey conducted by the National Survey of Student Engagement showed a self-reported average of only about fourteen hours per week spent studying, about half the hours that faculty say is necessary to do well in their classes. Assume four to five courses meeting for an average of three hours per week (and perfect attendance), and the average student is busy with academics for around twenty-six to twenty-nine hours per week. Even those hours of class time are structured to meet the students' preferences. Saturday classes no longer exist at most schools, and Friday classes are becoming rare because the weekend starts on Thursday night. Even Monday classes are being reduced. Or as a Duke administrator put it, "We've run out of classroom space between ten a.m. and two-thirty p.m. Tuesday through Thursday."

Using the student-teacher relationship as practice for the adult world of work? Among the many ways that colleges have evolved during the last three decades, the change in the student-teacher relationship appears to have been the most complete. In important respects, it is now the professors who must accommodate themselves to the preferences of the students, not the other way around. Requirements that used to be inflexible, such as the due date for papers, are now commonly revised when the student just can't get it done by then. Many professors permit quizzes or even final exams to be made up if missed—missed not because of an emergency at home or a fever of 104 degrees, but just, sort of, like, missed. At many schools, student evaluations of professors are now systematically collected and used as part of the tenure decision process, and being a tough teacher does not lead to enthusiastic evaluations. One instructor who gave his students a questionnaire asking what qualities they most valued in a teacher reports that the two most highly rated qualities were "entertaining" and "warm and friendly." One of the other options, "demanding," was not deemed desirable by a single student.

Teachers are even under pressure to accommodate students when it comes to right answers and wrong answers. Talk to any college teacher, and you will hear bemused accounts of encounters with students who think that the professor's criticisms of their work are "just your opinion," no more valid than the student's opinions. From a professor of psychology at San Diego State:

> I heard this complaint even when I corrected obvious errors like run-on sentences and incorrect punctuation, things that were clearly not a matter of opinion. Even multiple-choice tests weren't free from this kind of challenge. In one class, I decided it might be a good idea to review the correct answers to exam questions. . . . Almost immediately, several students began to argue with me about the questions, claiming that the answer they had chosen was right. Since there wasn't a grading mistake, I was forced to explain again why the answers were correct, but they continued to argue. . . .

The complaints become still louder and more frequent when a low grade is based on the professor's qualitative assessment of a student's term paper—now it's *really* just the professor's opinion—and it is not important that the professor's opinion was formed over years of advanced training and professional experience. On the contrary, invoking training and professional experience only antagonizes students. That way lies negative student evaluations, falling enrollment in your classes, and a session with the dean in which you are told to adjust to the new reality of the teacher-student relationship if you want to get tenure.

Nor is it possible for an individual teacher to do things the old-fashioned way, even if tenured. A history professor at Berkeley reports that she assigns today's students far fewer pages to read than in years past because she has discovered that it is futile: "They won't read them." The obvious retort is: If they don't read them, grade them accordingly. But that runs up against the pressures that make grade inflation so hard to reverse: If everyone else is giving out nothing but As and Bs, graduate schools and employers interpret Cs as the equivalent of a failing grade. There's no way for the professor to put on the transcript, "I grade the old-fashioned way. C represents average work." It is this reality—an honest C looks so bad that it may prevent a student from being accepted at medical school or law school—that finally drove one of the sternest of the old-school professors, Harvard's Harvey C. Mansfield (known to generations of students as Harvey C-minus Mansfield), to start giving out two grades: the inflated one for the transcript and the real one.

In this environment, the opportunities for learning of all kinds have diminished. Students learn less in the way of subject matter, but also less in the way of hard work, self-discipline, self-restraint, and respect for superior knowledge. This chapter is not the place to spin out the possible connections with the social phenomena—hooking up, date rape, binge drinking—that have been the subject of recent books about America's campuses. I am also wary of painting with too broad a brush. While changes such as grade inflation are almost universal, some schools have held the line on many standards of personal behavior and academic performance. But the larger and more impersonal the institution—and state universities routinely have more than 20,000 undergraduates—the harder it has been to hold the line. Admitting the exceptions, I put this proposition to you: For students whose parents are paying the bills, college life throughout much of the American system is not designed to midwife maturity but to prolong adolescence.

That proviso, "for students whose parents are paying the bills," raises the possibility that many of the problems of college life would go away if the parents were not paying the bills. College professors commonly observe that students who come to college after a hitch in the military or after working for several years, paying their own tuition, tend to take their courses more seriously and have a clearer sense of why they are taking a course than students who have come straight from high school. But the key factor may not be the money, but the greater maturity that has come during the intervening years. Students who are paying the bills but do not have that maturity can easily come to see education as a product they are buying. A professor at a community college, where many students come straight from high school but are paying their own way, described it this way:

By and large, students view themselves primarily as consumers who intended to study just a handful of hours a week for all their classes, and who expected, at a minimum, solid B's for their efforts. Students raised in a postmodern society of hyperconsumerism appear to want facile knowledge, served up in easily digestible, bite-sized chunks. . . . [They] pay their teachers to provide "knowledge," regardless of how superficial that knowledge might be. After all, how hard should a consumer have to work at buying something?

Being the person who pays the bills is no guarantee that college will be taken more seriously than it is taken by students who are not paying the bills. Whether any of this is a problem depends on what college is supposed to represent. If it is supposed to be a halcyon interlude before getting on with life as an adult, then there's no point in worrying about a prolonged adolescence. Many parents remember their own college years as a halcyon interlude, don't think it did them any harm in the long run, and are happy to finance the same experience for their children. But if the goal is to enable adolescents to become mature adults, parents should discard the idea that today's typical college can compete with going into the military or, for that matter, just moving out of the house and supporting themselves by working at any kind of job.

The Dark Side of the BA as a Norm

It is possible to accept all that I have presented as fact and still disagree with the proposition that too many people are going to college. The argument goes something like this:

> *The meaning of a college education has evolved since the nineteenth century. The traditional liberal education is still available for students who want it, but the curriculum is appropriately broader now, and includes many courses for vocational preparation that today's students want. Furthermore, intellectual requirements vary across majors. It may be true that few students can complete a major in economics or biology, but larger proportions can handle the easier majors.*
>
> *A narrow focus on curriculum also misses the important*

nonacademic functions of college. The lifestyle on today's campuses may leave something to be desired, but four years of college still give youngsters in late adolescence a chance to encounter different kinds of people, to discover new interests, and to decide what they want to make of their lives. And if it is true that some students spend too much of their college years partying, that was also true of many Oxford students in the eighteenth century. Lighten up.

If the only people we had to worry about were those who are on college campuses and doing reasonably well, this position would have something to be said for it. It does not address the issues of whether four years makes sense or whether a residential facility makes sense; nevertheless, college as it exists is not an intrinsically evil place for the students who are there and are coping academically. But there is the broader American society to worry about as well. However unintentionally, we have made something that is still inaccessible to a majority of the population—the BA—into a symbol of first-class citizenship. We have done so at the same time that other class divisions are becoming more powerful. Today's college system is implicated in the emergence of class-riven America.

The problem begins with the message sent to young people that they should aspire to college no matter what. Some politicians are among the most visible offenders, treating every failure to go to college as an injustice that can be remedied by increasing government help. American educational administrators reinforce the message by instructing guidance counselors to steer as many students as possible toward a college-prep track (more than 90 percent of high-school students report that their guidance counselors encouraged them to go to college). But politicians and educators are only following the lead of the larger culture. As long as it remains taboo to acknowledge that college is intellectually too demanding for most young people, we will continue to create crazily unrealistic expectations among the next generation. If "crazily unrealistic" sounds too strong, consider that more than 90 percent of high school seniors expect to go to college, and more than 70 percent of them expect to work in professional jobs.

One aspect of this phenomenon has been labeled *misaligned ambitions*, meaning that adolescents have career ambitions that are inconsistent with their educational plans. Data from the Sloan Study of Youth and Social Development conducted during the 1990s indicate that misaligned ambitions characterized more than half of all adolescents. Almost always, the misalignment is in the optimistic direction, as adolescents aspire to be attorneys or physicians without understanding the educational hurdles they must surmount to achieve their goals. They end up at a four-year institution not because that is where they can take the courses they need to meet their career goals, but because college is the place where BAs are handed out, and everyone knows that these days you've got to have a BA. Many of them drop out. Of those who entered a four-year college in 1995, only 58 percent had gotten their BA five academic years later. Another 14 percent were still enrolled. If we assume that half of that 14 percent eventually get their BAs, about a third of all those who entered college hoping for a BA leave without one.

If these numbers had been produced in a culture where the BA was a nice thing to have but not a big deal, they could be interpreted as the result of young adults deciding that they didn't really want a BA after all. Instead, these numbers were produced by a system in which having a BA is a very big deal indeed, and that brings us to the increasingly worrisome role of the BA as a source of class division. The

United States has always had symbols of class, and the college degree has always been one of them. But through the first half of the twentieth century, there were all sorts of respectable reasons why a person might not go to college—not enough money to pay for college; needing to work right out of high school to support a wife, parents, or younger siblings; or the commonly held belief that going straight to work was better preparation for a business career than going to college. As long as the percentage of college graduates remained small, it also remained true, and everybody knew it, that the majority of America's intellectually most able people did not have BAs.

Over the course of the twentieth century, three trends gathered strength. The first was the increasing proportion of jobs screened for high academic ability due to the advanced level of education they require—engineers, physicians, attorneys, college teachers, scientists, and the like. The second was the increasing market value of those jobs. The third was the opening up of college to more of those who had the academic ability to go to college, partly because the increase in American wealth meant that more parents could afford college for their children, and partly because the proliferation of scholarships and loans made it possible for most students with enough academic ability to go.

The combined effect of these trends has been to overturn the state of affairs that prevailed through World War II. Now the great majority of America's intellectually most able people do have a BA. Along with that transformation has come a downside that few anticipated. The acceptable excuses for not going to college have dried up. The more people who go to college, the more stigmatizing the failure to complete college becomes. Today, if you do not get a BA, many people assume it is because you are too dumb or too lazy. And all this because of a degree that seldom has an interpretable substantive meaning.

A few pages ago, I laid out the benign description of college as seen from the perspective of people lucky enough to have the brains and money to spend four years successfully on a college campus. Let's approach the situation from a different angle. Imagine that America had no system of postsecondary education and you were made a member of a task force assigned to create one from scratch. Ask yourself what you would think if one of your colleagues submitted this proposal:

> *First, we will set up a common goal for every young person that represents educational success. We will call it a BA. We will then make it difficult or impossible for most people to achieve this goal. For those who can, achieving the goal will take four years no matter what is being taught. We will attach an economic reward for reaching the goal that often has little to do with the content of what has been learned. We will lure large numbers of people who do not possess adequate ability or motivation to try to achieve the goal and then fail. We will then stigmatize everyone who fails to achieve it.*

What I have just described is the system that we have in place. There must be a better way.

4

America's Future Depends on How We Educate the Academically Gifted

T he last of the simple truths is easily misunderstood, so let me be clear at the outset: The proposition is not that America's future *should* depend on an elite that is educated to run the country, but that, whether we like it or not, America's future *does* depend on an elite that runs the country. The members of that elite are drawn overwhelmingly from among the academically gifted. We had better make sure that we do the best possible job of educating them.

The idea is instinctively unattractive. Educating people for leadership smacks of Plato's Guardians. Specifying academic giftedness puts logical-mathematical ability and linguistic ability on a pedestal, and it is not at all clear that these are the crucial abilities for leadership. What we need is leaders with more integrity, prudence, self-discipline, and moral courage, not smarter ones. What we need is more common sense in public life, not a bunch of overeducated intellectuals telling us what to do.

I agree with these sentiments, just as I agree with the late William F. Buckley that it would be better to be governed by the first

2,000 names in the Boston phone book than by the faculty of Harvard University. But the only members of the elite that we choose are elected officials, and they represent a small part of the totality of forces that shape our society. For practical purposes, the nation is run by an elite that we do not choose.

Narrowly defined, the unelected elite includes those who have risen to the top in jobs that have a direct impact on the nation's culture, economy, and politics. That definition includes the senior executives in the nation's largest corporations and financial institutions; the lawyers and judges who engage in the litigation that shapes our constitutional jurisprudence; the journalists whose bylines are found in the *New York Times, Washington Post, Wall Street Journal*, and the rest of the leading print media; the producers and writers who decide what will be covered on national television news programs and how it will be covered; the producers, directors, and writers who create the nation's films and television shows; and the most influential faculty in the nation's elite universities.

Broadly defined, the unelected elite includes those who have been successful locally. In the professions, it includes the nation's notably successful lawyers, physicians, engineers, physical scientists, social scientists, behavioral scientists, and tenured faculty. It includes the senior executives of small corporations and the owners of the most prosperous local businesses; the people who run the local banks, television stations, and newspapers; the administrators of school systems; the best elementary and secondary teachers; and the clergy of the major churches. It also includes a large number of housewives who lead civic, philanthropic, political, and religious activities in their towns and cities. In the aggregate, this broad elite has a massive effect on the nation's culture, economy, and politics, even though their individual day-to-day work does not have the same influence on the nation as the opinions of a famous syndicated columnist or the decisions of a *Fortune* 500 CEO.

Add them all up, and America's elite comprises a few million adults. But it is still an elite—a small fraction of our 300 million people. The good news is that America has gone further than any other country in opening admission to the elite to talented people whatever their origins. But that does not change the reality that a small proportion of the American population has a huge effect on our future. All we can do is try to educate members of the elite to be conscious of, and prepared to meet, the obligations that go with the roles they play. For years, we have not even thought about the nature of that task. It is time we did.

The Elite Is Already Smart. It Needs to Be Wise.

The place to begin is with my assertion that members of the elite are drawn from among the academically gifted. There are exceptions, of course, but put aside the empty-headed heirs and the empty-headed celebrities who are conspicuous but not that numerous. In every domain in American life where competition determines success, the people in the upper echelons are, with remarkable uniformity, able. The abilities that define *able* vary according to the task. The CEO of a successful corporation needs a package of abilities that is different from the package needed by the famous syndicated columnist, and their packages are in turn different from the one required by a Los Alamos physicist. But at the core of every package is "enough" academic ability.

The best analogy for thinking about the role of academic ability in career success is sociologist Steven Goldberg's: In most occupations, academic ability plays the same role in determining success that weight plays in determining the success of offensive tackles in the National Football League. The heaviest tackle is not necessarily the best. In fact, the correlation between weight and performance among NFL offensive tackles is probably quite small. Factors other than weight are decisive. But to have even a chance of getting the job, you had better weigh at least 300 pounds.

The intellectual equivalent of 300 pounds for most of the elite's occupations is an IQ score somewhere around 120. For the most intellectually demanding professions (e.g., physicist), 120 is on the low side. For others, it is on the high side. But it is a good ballpark figure for the academic ability needed to stand out in the jobs that are held by the people who run the country. For example, almost all of the nation's notably successful lawyers, physicians, engineers, physical scientists, social scientists, behavioral scientists, and tenured faculty have IQs of 120 or higher—a statement I can make because entry to all of those professions is screened by an academic filter that comes close to requiring an IQ that high, and I have further stipulated that I am talking about people who are notably successful. But scholarly investigations of the relationship of IQ to occupations also indicate that extremely large proportions of people who are notably successful in the rest of the elite roles I listed earlier have IQs of 120 and higher.

It's not surprising. We are not talking about geniuses. IQs of 120 and higher include almost 10 percent of the population. If we use ages twenty-five through sixty-four as our definition of the working-age population (not many people reach elite positions before age twenty-five), the top 10 percent in academic ability amounts to about 16 million Americans.

I will use the top 10 percent in academic ability as my definition of *gifted* (a much looser definition than the usual top 5 percent or top 2 percent), which means that when I say that the future of the nation depends on how we educate the academically gifted, I am not talking about a small cadre of students who go to the most prestigious schools.

By definition, the top 10 percent in academic ability included about 410,000 eighteen-year-olds in 2005, when about 1.5 million students enrolled as freshmen in four-year colleges. In the most recent *U.S. News & World Report* annual list, the top twenty national universities and top twenty liberal arts colleges combined enrolled only about 48,000 freshmen, and not all of them were in the top 10 percent. In round numbers, more than 90 percent of the academically gifted as I am using the word are *not* in the nation's most prestigious schools.

In short, we are talking about a lot of kids, and they are overwhelmingly to be found on the campuses of ordinary schools. What follows is not a discussion of how to educate Yale and Brown undergraduates, but how to educate a sizable proportion of undergraduates everywhere.

As I close this discussion of academic ability among the elite, let me offer two more clarifications to avoid misunderstandings: I am not saying that academic ability in the top 10 percent is absolutely essential to become a competent lawyer or journalist (for example). Rather, I am saying that almost all of the notably successful ones are in that category. Nor am I saying that everyone with academic ability in the top 10 percent is part of either elite. Most are not.

In what sense are we not doing a good job of educating the gifted now? The answer is complex, and does not necessarily coincide with the educational issues that most worry the parents of the gifted. Parents of the gifted are likely to be most upset during elementary school as they watch their children become bored and frustrated with classes that do not challenge them. They tend to become less worried during the high school years, as their children get access to honors courses, and then they breathe a sigh of relief when their children leave for a good college. In contrast, my worries center on the college years. The deficiencies of K–12 education for the gifted are severe in many public schools, but I will defer suggestions for remedying them to chapter 5.

Too few years of education is certainly not the problem. A large proportion of gifted children are born to parents who value their children's talent and do their best to see that it is realized. Most gifted children without such parents are recognized by someone somewhere along the educational line and pointed toward college. I already mentioned that about 90 percent of those in the top 10 percent of academic ability go to college. About 80 percent of the gifted get a BA. Of those, about half continue to some form of postgraduate education. If the measure is raw amount of education as measured by years in school, then the nation is doing fine with its next generation of gifted children. If the measure is the quality of their professional training, the nation is also doing fine. America's professional and graduate schools are the best in the world at turning out physicians who know their medicine, lawyers who know their law, and biologists who know their biology.

The problem with the education of the gifted involves not the amount of education nor their professional training, but their training as citizens. Those among the gifted who go on to become members of the elite make decisions that affect the lives of the rest of us. We need to structure their education so that they have the best possible chance to become not just knowledgeable but wise.

The encouragement of wisdom requires a special kind of education. It requires mastery of the tools of verbal expression—not because the gifted will need them to communicate in daily life, but because they are indispensable for precise thinking at an advanced level. It requires mastery of the analytical building blocks for making sound judgments, because the elite makes judgments, intentionally or unconsciously, that affect the lives of people far beyond their family and friends. The encouragement of wisdom requires extended study of philosophy, because it is not enough that gifted children grow up to be nice. They must know what it means to be good. Finally and indispensably, the encouragement of wisdom requires that we teach students to recognize their own intellectual limits and fallibilities—teach them humility.

In a generic sense, I am calling for a revival of the classical understanding of a liberal education at the college level, serving its classic purpose: to prepare an elite to do its duty. But I am not trying to make a case for obligatory study of Greek and Latin or for a St. John's College curriculum that consists exclusively of the classics. Here in more detail are the themes that I consider central to the education of the gifted:

RIGOR IN VERBAL EXPRESSION

Verbal expression is what the elite does. A comparatively few members of the elite—for example, some types of scientists, physicians, and artists—exercise advanced physical skills, but usually the physical aspect of the elite's work consists of reading, tapping on keyboards, listening, and talking. Hence the importance of verbal skills.

The acquired verbal skills of gifted American students have declined dramatically, as illustrated by the trends in the SAT-Verbal test. Consider a score of 700 or higher on the SAT-Verbal, the kind of score needed to have a good chance of getting into a highly selective college. In the first year for which data are available, 1967, about 29,000 students got such a score. Since almost all students who are capable of getting such a high score have been taking the SAT since the 1960s, it is possible to treat this number as a rough proportion of all seventeen-year-olds. As of 1967, it worked out to 1 out of every 120. When the SAT scores bottomed out in 1980–1981, that ratio had dropped to 1 out of every 400. It has recovered only modestly since then. The ratio of those getting 700+ SAT-Verbal scores in 1994, the last year before the test was recentered, was 1 out of 313. It is probably about the same today, although there's no way of knowing without having access to the College Board's raw data (a 700 SAT-Verbal score on the pre-recentered test now is equivalent to 760).

This decline cannot be blamed on changes in the SAT pool. It is based on all seventeen-year-olds. Some sort of failure to educate the gifted is to blame. Nor can the failure to recover from the decline be blamed on a completely ineffectual educational system. The great SAT score decline of the 1960s and 1970s resulted in widespread demands for better education—and, in mathematics, those demands were met. When the last SAT before recentering was administered in 1994, the percentage of seventeen-year-olds getting 700+ in the SAT-Math had not only recovered from its low in the early 1980s, it had reached an all-time high.

Why didn't SAT-Verbal scores recover as well? The most straightforward explanation is that parental demands to raise the bar for mathematics performance resulted in real toughening of the math curriculum, whereas demands to raise the bar for verbal performance did not. With math, rigor is accepted as part of the package. No one thinks that the purpose of a good advanced calculus class is to teach the students how to be creative. They are supposed to learn the mathematics of advanced calculus. But the teaching of the humanities and social sciences in the public schools continues to reflect a mind-set that took hold as part of the progressive education movement. Persnickety insistence on correct spelling, grammar, syntax, and logic is out. Creative self-expression is in. The use of the word *rigorous* with the phrase *verbal expression* is oxymoronic in most public schools.

In reality, verbal expression is subject to as much rigor as mathematical expression. Rigor starts with correct understanding of the meanings of individual words, as well as their correct spellings. It proceeds to an understanding of the parts of speech and how they come together in the rules of grammar. Rigor then requires an understanding of how sentences are structured to convey meaning—syntax. Independently of grammar and syntax, rigor in verbal expression requires mastery of the principles of reasoning and their relationship to language. This mastery must include the ability to recognize the basic types of fallacy. Finally, rigor in verbal expression requires an understanding of the principles of rhetoric, both as a tool for expression and as a protection against being misled by rhetoric that is misused.

Learning this material has nothing to do with the student's creativity or imagination. A student cannot have an opinion about whether a sentence that contains a fallacy is false. He needs to learn that it *is* false, as a construction of words. Whether the sentiment that the writer of the words had in mind is true is another issue. Understanding the distinction between *true* positions and *correct statements* of those positions is part of wisdom. Understanding the distinction between *correct* statements of positions and *persuasive* statements of positions is another part of wisdom. Both of those understandings depend on rigorous training in verbal expression.

Learning verbal expression in an advanced form is intellectually demanding work that only a small number of students can handle (take the intellectual requirements for understanding the college-level texts in chapter 3 and jack them up a few notches). But most students do not need to learn verbal expression in an advanced form. Hardly any of the speaking and writing that people do from day to day requires detailed knowledge of grammar and syntax. Hardly any of their thoughts must be subjected to close semantic and logical examination. Return to our electrician from chapter 3. He has to know how to do things right, using the right tools and the right procedures. He has to be able to read instructional material. He has to be able to communicate effectively with coworkers and customers. None of this requires rigor in verbal expression. But suppose he decides to become a manager instead. At the lower levels of management, rigor in verbal expression is seldom more important than it is for the electrician. But as a manager climbs higher, the decisions he has to make about personnel, allocation of resources, and the organization's objectives require increasingly difficult choices among options. Organizing and formulating those options precisely becomes more and more important. Rigor in verbal expression is as indispensable a tool for those tasks as a pair of pliers is for the electrician.

RIGOR IN FORMING JUDGMENTS

To be in a position of power means that what you do affects people beyond your immediate family and friends, and the consequences of failing to do the right thing escalate accordingly. From the decisions of a George W. Bush about whether the nation should go to war to the decisions of a Ken Lay about how Enron should structure its accounting system to the decisions of a Don Hewitt about how to frame a story on *60 Minutes*, members of the elite make judgments that affect the culture and nation, sometimes profoundly. Making those judgments is more complicated than deciding what feels right.

Sound judgment has four components. One is unteachable. Some people have a flair for making sense of complicated situations in the same way that some people have a flair for playing the violin. This flair for making sound decisions is surely correlated with academic ability, but is something distinct from it as well. When people talk about "common sense," they are capturing part of it. Aristotle's discussion of *phronesis*, "practical wisdom," relates to this skill. The second component of sound judgment is the appropriate application of logic to the problem, fostered by rigor in verbal expression. The other two components that go into sound judgment are the evaluation of data and pattern recognition, and both have teachable aspects.

The evaluation of data lends itself to the most directly teachable techniques. No matter how highly charged an issue might be, its components can be disaggregated into specific bits of information and the specific claims that are being made about what those bits mean. These in turn lend themselves to appraisal by explicit standards of reliability and validity. Sometimes the data are qualitative and the techniques for evaluating them must be qualitative (rigor in verbal expression is crucial in these cases). But many social and political issues, and almost all economic issues, are also informed by quantitative data and analysis. You saw an example of just such an issue in chapter 2, when I discussed the evidence about preschool interventions for disadvantaged children. Responding to children in need is about as instinctive as human responses get, and as emotionally charged. But deciding how to use scarce resources to help disadvantaged children is not a matter of caring. It is a matter of deciding what works and what doesn't.

Over the last half-century, social scientists have developed their quantitative tools to the point that hard evidence can be brought to bear on such questions. But with that progress goes a new responsibility: teaching the average college graduate how to appraise that evidence. I had to censor my discussion of the evidence on preschool interventions (using percentile points instead of standard deviations to describe the magnitude of the effects was just one of many ways) because even though I know that the average IQ of my readers is high, and that almost all of you have BAs, I could not assume that more than a minority of you has ever taken a college-level course in statistics. If you want to be able to judge whether I am right or the educational romantics are right about the results of preschool interventions for poor children—an important disagreement about an important and live issue in today's America—you've got to have a thorough grounding in statistics. That same grounding is required to make sense of claims about global warming, rising income inequality, or the effects of secondhand smoke. There's no other option if you want to make informed judgments.

Widespread statistical illiteracy among the gifted is cause for immediate concern because none of us, no matter how thorough our training, has the time to assess the data independently on every topic. We all have to rely on the quality of the information we get from the media—and, as of today, that quality is terrible. The next time you hear or read a news account of findings on global warming, rising income inequality, the effects of secondhand smoke, the effectiveness of preschool interventions, or of No Child Left Behind, pay special attention to the technical material included in the story. You will not need a degree in statistics or research methodology to see the amateurishness of the scientific reporting from even the biggest news outlets, written by reporters who attended the most prestigious colleges. Sometimes it fails to convey the information we need to know. Sometimes it is misleading. Too often it is simply wrong.

Pattern recognition, the fourth component of sound decision making, is why history is such an essential part of a liberal education—why, in the famous words of George Santayana, those who cannot remember the past are condemned to repeat it. Pattern recognition refers to the ability to see the relevance of other nonidentical situations. It is inextricably linked with experience. A child can play wonderful chess at age seven or eight just by knowing the tactical techniques of chess and having an abundance of raw talent for the game. What takes the prodigy to the grandmaster level in his teens is his accumulated exposure to thousands of positions combined with the ability to see the similarities of those positions to the one he faces in the present game. Similarly, a young physician can be a technically proficient diagnostician the day he finishes his internship, but he cannot become a great diagnostician except by accumulating the experience that is the foundation of pattern recognition.

Both of these examples illustrate how experience can be personal and vicarious. Personal experience is important, but the chess prodigy studies thousands of games played by the great players of the past to gain vicarious experience. The physician who wants to become a great diagnostician immerses himself in medical journals and texts long after medical school to build up his vicarious experience and thereby enhance his capacity for pattern recognition.

In all of the great cultural, political, and economic issues of the day, the study of history is how we develop vicarious experience, and that's why extensive study of history must be part of a liberal education. I do not mean one required survey course, but closer to half a dozen. The rewards of studying history are not abstract. The very creation of the United States is a case in point. The Founders did not imagine that they could make up a Constitution in a vacuum. They consciously undertook a study of democracies and republics from ancient Greece and Rome up through their own time, analyzing the reasons why each had collapsed. The mechanisms they devised— checks and balances, separation of powers, and the rest—were directly influenced by that analysis.

RIGOR IN THINKING ABOUT VIRTUE AND THE GOOD

From Harvard's founding in 1636 until the Civil War, the chief purpose of American colleges was to teach undergraduates about the meaning of life. A major part of that endeavor was devoted to study of Christian theology. The secular part comprised the humanities—the study of philosophy, literature, history, and, in some schools, music and art. After the Civil War, as American colleges became less tightly tied to religion, the administrators and faculty of these institutions continued to believe that it was possible to offer students a coherent, disciplined curriculum for examining the meaning of life through the humanities. Students no longer took exactly the same courses in the same order as they had done in antebellum universities, but most colleges required students to take an extensive core curriculum that ensured exposure to the greatest work in the humanities.

Underlying this function of college was the recognition that certain issues are so fundamental to the human condition that people *must* think about them. The yearning for transcendence is the overarching example. Anthony Kronman, whose 2007 book *Education's End* is to university education what E. D. Hirsch's *Cultural Literacy* is to elementary and secondary education, expressed it beautifully:

[The humanities] invite—they compel—us to confront the truth about ourselves and help us to inhabit with greater understanding the disjointed condition of longing and defeat that defines the human condition. Achilles' reflections on honor and memory and the fleeting beauty of youth; Shakespeare's defense of love against the powers of "sluttish time"; Kant's struggle to put our knowledge of certain things on an unchallengeable foundation so as to place the knowledge of others forever beyond reach; Caravaggio's painting of the sacrifice of Isaac, which depicts a confusion of loves that defeats all understanding; and so on endlessly through the armory of humanistic works: the subject is always the same. The subject is always man, whose nature it is to yearn to be more than he is.

For an eloquent statement of the case for liberal education in the humanities, Kronman's book is the place to go. Here, I take up one corner of the topic, the role of college in providing a disciplined, coordinated study of the question that every college student is of an age to ask: What does it mean to live a good human life?

I am happy to report that today's gifted students are, for the most part, nice. Such is the impression of someone who has spent a fair amount of time on campuses over the past twenty years. The students I encounter at these schools are not sexist, racist, or homophobic. In conversation, they are earnest about social problems. They want to be generous to those who are less fortunate. They say please and thank you.

But being nice is not being good. Living a nice life is not living a good life. One of the special tasks in the education of the gifted is to steep them in the study of what good means—*good* as it applies to virtue, and *the Good* as a way of thinking about how to live a human life.

Teaching virtue. Virtue by what definition? It sounds like a daunting question. It is not. The great ethical systems of the world are in such remarkable agreement on the core issues that, practically speaking, any of them will do. I could make that case in terms of the major religious traditions, but let me use instead the world's two most influential secular ethical systems, Aristotelian (conceding Aristotle's debt to Plato) and Confucian. The proposition is that adults observing either system will behave indistinguishably in the ways that matter most, because they have such similar understandings of virtue.

Start with Aristotle and the four cardinal virtues, approximately translated as temperance, courage, practical wisdom, and justice. They are called cardinal, derived from the Latin *cardo*, meaning hinge, because they are pivotal: All the other virtues depend on them. Temperance is pivotal because, without it, any subsidiary virtue will be ignored when it competes with natural appetites. Courage is pivotal because no virtue is sustained in the face of adversity without it. Practical wisdom—rightly assessing the consequences of a course of action—is pivotal because it is the precondition for behaving in other virtuous ways (you may want to be compassionate, for example, but without practical wisdom you may behave in ways that cause suffering rather than relieve it). Justice—as defined by Aristotle, giving everyone his rightful due—is pivotal because it is a precondition for behaving in other virtuous ways (for example, compassion rightly takes different forms for people in different circumstances).

Now turn to Confucius and the central virtue in his system, *ren*, the summation of all subsidiary virtues. *Ren* translates literally as humaneness or benevolence, but the Confucian conception of *ren* is richer than either word conveys. *Ren* incorporates the idea of reciprocity (a form of the Golden Rule) that overlaps with Aristotle's concept of justice. *Ren* incorporates courage. Confucius is emphatic about the need for temperance and self-control. And one of the chief requirements of *ren* is the considered, accurate appraisal of consequences that Aristotle described as practical wisdom. Like Aristotle, Confucius emphasized that the possession of virtue is a matter not just of right understanding, but of daily behavior that corresponds to right understanding. Aristotle and Confucius were in agreement that those with the most power have an obligation to set the right example for others.

Writing two centuries apart in cultures unaware of each other's existence, Aristotle and Confucius laid down systems that would dominate their respective worlds for the next two millennia. The differences between the two systems are associated with profound differences in the cultures (more on that presently). But from day to day, these differences are trivial in comparison with their similarities. If your children grow up to be courageous, temperate, able to think clearly about the consequences of their actions, to be concerned with the welfare of others, with a sense of obligation to set a good example for others in their own behavior and to accord to others their rightful due, do you really care whether they were raised to be good Aristotelians or good Confucians?

To put it in terms of American education, it makes no practical difference whether a student comes out of a school that has done a good job of teaching Aristotelian virtue or Confucian virtue; or, moving away from the secular, whether it has done a good job of teaching Buddhist virtue, Christian virtue, Judaic virtue, Islamic virtue, or Hindu virtue. Each of these traditions has historical baggage that we may worry about (e.g., the Inquisition, Islamic radicalism), but the core meaning of virtue in all of the traditions, effectively transmitted, will produce people who are virtuous in similar ways.

Teaching about the Good. For answering the question "What does it mean to live a good human life?" thinking about virtue is not enough. It is also necessary to think about what human beings are made for—in Aristotelian terms, to think about the excellence peculiar to human beings that we should strive to realize. In broader terms, what is the nature of human happiness? Here, the great traditions diverge. By focusing on the importance of the unique human capacity for rational thought, Aristotelianism, with an eventual push from Aquinas, contributed to the development of Western individualism that inspires the young to go off to fulfill their potential, and, in the process of doing so, to roil the established ways of doing things. Confucianism locates happiness in the matrix of human relationships that make up family and community and is tailor-made for societies that value stability and close familial and community ties.

When it comes to thinking about the nature of human happiness, I am a multiculturalist. The great traditions are not interchangeable. Each has identified truths about the human condition that the other traditions have not understood as deeply, and anyone who is trying to achieve a personal understanding of what constitutes happiness would do well to tap into the wisdom of all of them. The problem arises when education teaches none of these traditions.

This is one instance in which nostalgia about education in the good old days has some justification: Once upon a time, American schools indoctrinated their students with admirable perspectives on virtue and happiness. There are many ways to make that point. For example, the McGuffey Readers, which formed the elementary-school reading of generations of American children, are crammed with moral instruction and cautionary tales that reflect coherent understandings of virtue and the nature of human happiness. But let me reflect for a moment on another example, the way that schools treated sports.

A hundred years ago, the phrase "It's not whether you win or lose, but how you play the game" was not a cliché that people mocked. People really believed it. The phrases "a good sport" and "a bad loser" had meaning, and those meanings were rooted in moral precepts. Fictional athletic heroes Frank Merriwell and Dink Stover were moral paragons, and the novels portraying them were runaway bestsellers of juvenile fiction. Educators brought this view of sports-as-morality-play to the conduct of games at school. Agreeing with Aristotle that virtue is acquired by becoming a habit, and habits are formed by daily practice, they saw sports as an arena for practicing virtues—fair play, courage in adversity, loyalty to teammates, modesty in victory, dignity in defeat. Sports were also seen as a way to let students understand the valid sources of human satisfaction—doing one's best is a source of self-respect, regardless of whether one wins or loses, and there can be satisfaction in winning only if the winning has been accomplished the right way. Athletics were a tool for moral instruction.

That consensus is gone now. Insofar as educators think about the educational role of sports within the school, it is likely to be with regard to self-esteem, leading to worries that students who lose a game in PE class will have lowered self-esteem. Meanwhile, the high school football and basketball teams in the same school system may be led by coaches who teach their players that "Winning isn't everything; it's the only thing," and "Show me a good loser and I'll show you a loser." There are exceptions, but, by and large, sports exist in a moral void where no one is thinking hard about the nature of virtue, the nature of human happiness, and the school's role in imparting sound understandings to children.

The same void extends throughout the curriculum and the school day. Today's public schools (and many of today's secular private schools) tell children to be nice but not how to be good. It tells children to be happy but does nothing to help children think about what *happiness* means. It is a problem that extends from kindergarten through college, and one that affects children at all levels of academic ability. One of the reasons for using the Core Knowledge curriculum in the elementary schools is that its readings expose elementary-school students to at least some of the moral instruction that has been stripped from American education.

I am nonetheless discussing the problem here, in terms of its effects on the gifted, because of the elite's special influence on the cultural milieu. What we see on television and in films, hear in our music, read in our newspapers and books, is all produced by members of the elite. The content is filtered through their impoverished understandings of virtue and the Good, or through a sensibility that is innocent of any such understandings. The depressing reality is that hardly any of the people who have such enormous influence on our culture have ever been in a school that made sure they thought about these issues. Most of the members of today's elite are ethically illiterate. They are not bad people. They are not indifferent. They have done as well as most human beings do when they try to think through questions involving virtue and happiness unaided. The problem is that they have been given no help in tapping the magnificent body of thought on these issues that *Homo sapiens* has already produced.

Instead, if they have gone to a typical college, they have imbibed the reigning ethical doctrine of contemporary academia: nonjudgmentalism. They have been taught not just that they should be tolerant of different ways of living, but that it is wrong to make judgments about the relative merit of different ways of living. It is the inverse of rigor in thinking about virtue and the Good—a task that, above all else, requires the formation of considered judgments.

Since we are starting from scratch, our ambitions for encouraging rigor in thinking about virtue and the Good should be modest. It would constitute a major step forward if the typical gifted student emerged from college with a reasoned appreciation of just two things:

Being virtuous is hard. It is not enough to behave pleasantly toward others. Behaving in ways that conduce to the good ends you seek takes measured thoughtfulness—Aristotle's practical wisdom. Even when the others are intimately known to us as spouses, children, siblings, or parents, we must face difficult trade-offs between short-term and long-term effects, between plusses and minuses ("Should I force my aging father to move into a nursing home?"). As soon as the others become even a little more distant, the difficulties multiply. All the idiosyncrasies of individuals come into play, but now we are in the dark. When the decisions we must make affect large numbers of people, we no longer have the option of making case-by-case decisions. Our only alternative is to draw upon principles of right behavior and principles of human flourishing. It is folly to formulate those principles and to make those decisions without having drawn upon the wisest who have come before us.

Seeking the Good for oneself is both important and feasible. For those who are observant members of any of the great religions, an articulated conception of the Good and how it should shape their lives is constantly before them. My second modest ambition for the gifted focuses on those who are secular. For them, it is easy to leave college ambitious to be a good person but without any understanding that a difference exists between trying to do good for others and seeking the Good for oneself. They should be aware that seeking the Good is something that can be addressed in secular as well as religious terms, that thinking about it is crucial to their future happiness—and that people even smarter than they are have written helpfully about it in the past.

HUMILITY

Today's gifted students may be nice people (usually), but they are not exempt from the unlovely attitudes and behaviors of college students that I discussed in chapter 3. They often feel no sense of responsibility for a disappointing grade, but are affronted by it. Often, they do not diffidently approach the professor asking if they may submit a revised version of the term paper, but confront the professor with a demand that the grade be raised because the professor failed to recognize the brilliance of their insights. Another topic in chapter 3, the light workload at college, also applies forcefully to the gifted. I exempt those who are majoring in mathematics, engineering, and the hard sciences, but for the gifted who go into the humanities or social sciences, college is pretty easy. It is not a new problem. "The hardest thing about Harvard is getting in" was already a commonplace in the early 1960s. But whenever it began, it certainly remains true today: Talented students in the humanities and social sciences can often get by without coming close to hitting their intellectual limits.

Gifted students experience this undemanding education under the care of parents and teachers who have, for the most part, accepted the proposition that the key to successful development of children is high self-esteem and therefore are fearful of wounding them. The self-esteem movement, which got its start at the end of the 1960s with the publication of Nathaniel Branden's *Psychology of Self-Esteem*, could have been a force for good if it had focused on self-esteem as Branden described it—an internalized sense of self-responsibility and self-sufficiency. But the movement focused instead on *having* a favorable opinion of oneself, independently of objective justification for that favorable opinion. Children were to be praised, because praise fosters self-esteem. If criticism were unavoidable, the criticism should be cocooned in layers of praise, because criticism undermines self-esteem. Classroom competitions should be avoided, because they damage the self-esteem of the losers.

From the 1970s through the 1990s, low self-esteem took on the aura of a meta-explanation. California went so far as to establish a task force on self-esteem, which predictably concluded in its 1989 report that "[M]any, if not most, of the major problems plaguing society have roots in the low self-esteem of many of the people who make up society." And since low self-esteem was the problem, high self-esteem was the solution. Psychological health, high educational performance, earnings as an adult—whatever the desired outcome, higher self-esteem would help produce it.

Over the last several years, the self-esteem movement has been debunked in the technical literature. The landmark change in scholarly opinion occurred in 2003 when a review of the 15,000 studies that had been written on the relationship of self-esteem to the development of children concluded that improving self-esteem does not raise grades, career achievement, or have any other positive effect.

Other recent findings not only debunk the self-esteem myth but provide new ways of thinking about why gifted children are turning out the way they do. Contemporary parents almost reflexively tell their children that they are smart, in contrast to an earlier era when parents were worried about giving their children big heads. But according to recent experiments, praising children for being smart backfires. Given a new task, children praised for being smart tend to choose the easier alternative. In a meta-analysis of 150 praise studies, other scholars concluded that praise makes children averse to risk and decreases their sense of autonomy. These scholars found consistent correlations between repeated praise and "shorter task persistence, more eye-checking with the teacher, and inflected speech such that answers have the intonation of questions." And this finding begins to bring us back to college students angrily demanding that professors raise their grades: Researchers are discovering that the more children are praised, the more important it becomes for them to maintain their image. Their goal becomes to protect themselves, not to outshine others through superior achievement.

I have no statistics on the percentage of gifted children who are raised in homes where they have been constantly praised for being smart and at the same time have not been strenuously challenged academically. It should go without saying that this description does not fit all gifted children or perhaps even most. But it corresponds with the milieu in which many gifted children grow up, with the observed behavior of many gifted children in college, and with the current state of knowledge about the effects of praise.

There is a healthier alternative—healthier for gifted children and for the society that some of them will run as adults. Since they are in fact academically gifted, it is fine to tell them that. Trying to hide their academic ability from them would be futile anyway. But they must also be told explicitly, forcefully, and repeatedly that their intellectual talent is a gift that they have done nothing to deserve. They are not superior human beings, but very, very lucky ones. They should feel humbled by their good luck.

At that point, praising them for actual accomplishment produced by hard work does no harm. But even then, we know from our own experience that the mentors who made a difference in our lives were seldom the ones who praised us effusively but those who demanded our best. At the end of it all, the praise may have been no more than the mentor looking up from our last, best effort and saying "Not bad." That's the praise we still cherish years later. That's what today's gifted students will cherish if we give them teachers who demand their best.

This healthier alternative also means making sure that at some point every gifted student fails in some academic task. There is no sadism in this, but an urgent need for our luckiest children to gain perspective on themselves and on their fellows. As matters stand, many among the gifted who manage to avoid serious science and math never take a course from kindergarten through graduate school that is so tough that they have to say to themselves, "I can't do this." Lacking that experience, too many gifted graduates are not conscious of their own limits. They may acknowledge them theoretically, but they don't feel them in their gut. They don't know, as an established fact, that there are some things they just aren't smart enough to figure out.

Everybody else knows that for a fact. Children of low academic ability have to deal with that knowledge in elementary school. Children of average academic ability have to deal with it in high school. Children of moderately above-average academic ability have to deal with it in their postsecondary education. Even the children with stratospherically high academic ability who get deep enough into mathematics have to deal with it. It is said that there comes a point in every mathematics student's education when he hears himself saying to the teacher, "I think I understand"—and that's the point at which he has hit the wall. Making sure that all gifted students hit their own personal walls is crucial for developing their empathy with the rest of the world. When they see their less lucky peers struggle academically, they need to be able to say "I know how it feels"—and be telling the truth.

But empathy is not the chief reason that gifted students need to hit the wall. It is even more important that they achieve humility. A wonderful maxim is attributed to George Christian, one of Lyndon Johnson's press secretaries: "No one should be allowed to work in the West Wing of the White House who has not suffered a major disappointment in life." The responsibility of working there was too great, Christian thought, to be entrusted to people who weren't painfully aware how badly things can go wrong. The same principle applies to those who will become members of America's elite. No one among the gifted should be allowed to rise to a position of influence without knowing what it feels like to fail. The experience of internalized humiliation is a prerequisite for humility.

When reading an argument in favor of special attention for the academically gifted, wariness is appropriate. The gifted disproportionately come from homes in which they already have everything going for them—loving parents, a big house in a peaceful neighborhood, good schools, money for college. I hope it is clear that this argument for special treatment of the gifted has nothing to do with providing yet more advantages for the little darlings. Since they include the people who will end up running the country, it is time for the educational system to start holding their feet to the fire.

Letting Change Happen

I n K–12 education, the educational romantics are trying to do what cannot be done and are neglecting what can be done. Big improvements, things we know we can do, are both feasible and affordable. In postsecondary education, an archaic system is under pressure from the market and from new technology, and much can be accomplished with strategic prodding at vulnerable points. I begin with K–12, then turn to postsecondary education.

The Funnel

For all of the seven abilities, education's potential role is shaped like a funnel. For those who have the least ability, education's potential is represented by the narrow end of the funnel, and there's not much room to do anything. As ability rises, the potential role of education expands. For those at the highest level of ability, the width of the funnel is limited only by the breadth of the knowledge available to be taught. The funnel applies to education of all kinds, whether its goal is to teach someone to play basketball, play the violin, draw a picture, make a sale, meditate, read, or do math.

When it comes to reading or doing math, the educational romantics have refused to accept that the funnel analogy applies. Over the
past forty years they have obsessed about how to make large gains in
reading and math at the bottom end of the funnel, where only marginal gains are possible. Ending that obsession is the first step
toward better K–12 education.

It is not going to be easy. The insistence that we can dramatically
improve the academic performance of low-ability children has an
almost religious tenacity. It has to be broken, and, ultimately, the only
way to do that is with evidence. I know how naive this sounds. Who
but a social scientist would begin a chapter on how to improve education with a recommendation for more studies? But it is not just ideas
that have consequences. Facts are stubborn things, and they too
eventually must have consequences. Two sets of facts need to be
established in a way that the romantics can no longer ignore.

Make the Probabilities Public

The standard for assessing educational achievement for K–12 is the
National Assessment of Educational Progress (NAEP). Policy
debates that have led to huge consequences (the passage of No Child
Left Behind is a case in point) have been framed in terms of what
NAEP shows about the condition of American education. But as matters stand, the measures we take from NAEP float free of any measure of what we can reasonably expect. In chapter 2, I pointed out
that we have no idea whether a 26 percent failure rate for NAEP's
eighth-grade Basic reading level (or any other failure rate for any
grade) is good or bad. If a child needs linguistic ability at the 26th
percentile to have a fifty-fifty chance of passing the Basic level, then
the best educational system in the world will have about a 26 percent

failure rate. So let us find out whether the failure rates we observe are signs of success or signs of problems. Let us link our measures of educational achievement with measures of academic ability.

The task is technically simple. Give a large sample of six-year-olds a good test of linguistic ability that requires no reading skills. Tests of this sort already exist, with the Peabody Picture Vocabulary Test being one of the best and most widely used. Then give the same children NAEP's reading test when they reach the fourth, eighth, and twelfth grades. Make sure that the students who are tested come from a range of schools that include the very best ones. Prepare a graph in which the horizontal axis is linguistic ability measured at age six and the vertical axis is percentage of children passing the Basic reading level. Do the same thing with a measure of logical-mathematical ability and NAEP's math test. You will have your answers.

If it were to be found that students with below-average linguistic ability coming into first grade have widely different probabilities of passing the Basic reading level, and those probabilities depend on what school they went to, then we would have a basis for improving the education of low-ability students: Just determine what the schools with the high pass rates are doing right, and make all schools do the same thing. But if instead it turns out that reading achievement among low-ability students averages out to about what one would have predicted from their linguistic ability measured at school entry *no matter what schools they attend* (except at the worst inner-city schools—I always except them), and the same is true of math achievement among students who enter school with low scores in a test of logical-mathematical ability, then we can stop obsessing. There's not much that even the best schools can do to raise the reading and math achievement of low-ability children.

We do not need to wait for years for such a study to be completed. Thousands of six-year-olds are given the Peabody Picture Vocabulary Test every year, just as thousands of six-year-olds are given tests that measure logical-mathematical ability. All that the government or a private foundation needs to do is engage the research companies that administer NAEP to identify such children who are now in fourth, eighth, and twelfth grades and give them NAEP's tests. We could have the results within two years after the contract is signed.

Establish the Limits of the Possible

After the results of the study come in (which I predict will verify what we learned from the Coleman Report more than forty years ago), educational romantics will point out that even though schools did not make much difference in the achievement of low-ability students, there is nonetheless a wide range of reading and math achievement among children with the same test score in first grade. For example, it will be found that some students at the 26th percentile on linguistic ability at age six scored at the 50th or 60th percentile of reading achievement at age thirteen. The romantics' conclusion: See? Some kids make a big jump. We *can* improve achievement among low-ability students; it's just that even our best schools aren't nearly as good as schools could be. Hence my second proposal, for a study that would be the most expensive educational demonstration project in history and would take as much as fifteen or twenty years from beginning to end. I state it in the form of a challenge to everyone who is convinced that we can teach low-ability children far more than we are currently teaching them: Put up or shut up.

Seven of the ten largest American foundations, with combined assets of $81 billion as of 2007, give grants for education. Other large foundations such as the Walton Family Foundation ($1.4 billion endowment) have taken K–12 education as a top funding priority. All of these foundations are associated with the romantic view of what is possible. The experiment that will prove people like me to be wrong would probably cost well over $100 million, but any one of those foundations could fund it if it wished, and a consortium of them could easily fund it. Here is the proposal:

Select children who test low in academic ability but are not clinically retarded—say, children with measured IQs from 80 to 95, which demarcate the 10th to 37th percentiles. Make the number of children in the study large enough that the results cannot be explained away as accidents of small samples. Then provide these groups of children with the best elementary education that anyone knows how to provide. Build new facilities or renovate existing ones. Hire the best teachers and create a model curriculum. Measure how well the children are doing at the end of elementary school, and compare their progress with that of other children matched for IQ, family background, and whatever other variables are considered important.

The experiment should consist of several groups. One group of children could be selected at infancy and given highly enriched preschool programs, followed by outstanding elementary school programs, while another group is selected at age five, to explore how much difference the preschool experience might have made. One group of children could be drawn from a high-poverty neighborhood, but the control group should go to a functional urban school, not one of the horrific ones. The point of the experiment is not to prove that we can do much better for low-ability children than the worst inner-city schools do now (of course we can), but to prove that we can do much better for them than average schools do now. Since a standard excuse for failed experiments is that the effects of the intervention were swamped by the competing effects of poverty, racism, or neighborhood environment, at least one experimental group should consist of middle-class Anglo-European children whose only problem is low ability.

The people who conduct the experiment should be free to use any teaching techniques, any class sizes, any amount of one-on-one tutoring, any kind of technological aid. They shouldn't worry about making the program financially affordable for wider application, but instead bring to bear every resource that anyone can think of, at whatever cost, that will maximize the education that these children acquire. Or to put it another way, their mission is to conduct the experiment in such a way that, if it fails to produce success, there will be no excuses. Only three ground rules are nonnegotiable:

- The organization that selects the experimental and control samples and tests the children must be completely independent of and isolated from the organization that conducts the experiment.
- The design must protect against teaching to the test and test-practice effects.
- The design must include a test for fadeout, conducted three years after the experimental education ends.

Anyone issuing a challenge has to put himself on the line, so here are my predictions. On measures involving interpersonal and intrapersonal ability, I expect statistically significant but substantively modest gains. On measures of factual knowledge, the experimental group will score dramatically higher than the members of the comparison group, perhaps 30-plus percentile points higher (technically, more than a standard deviation). On measures of reading and math achievement, the differences will be no more than 15 to 20 percentile points (about half a standard deviation). Three years after the experiment ends, all of the differences will have shrunk. The differences in reading and math will be no more than 8 to 12 percentile points (no more than a third of a standard deviation) and may have disappeared altogether.

More formally, I predict that the magnitude of each academic effect will be a function of the g loading of the measure. Measures of retention of simple factual material have the lowest g loadings and will show the largest gains. For highly g-loaded measures such as reading comprehension and math, what has been accomplished by the last half-century of preschool and elementary-school interventions will be shown to be about as good as we can do, no matter how much money we spend.

A few hundred million dollars and fifteen or twenty years seems like a lot of money and a long time to demonstrate something that, in my judgment, we already know. But if I am wrong, the payoff will be incalculable. Even if I am right, the payoff is large. Many useful educational innovations are bound to come out of such an intensive and wide-ranging effort. And there is immense value just in establishing the outer limits of what can be accomplished with the current state of knowledge. The people who create educational policy have managed to ignore the results of previous interventions, grasping at every positive fragment of evidence while ignoring the brunt of the findings, saying that the next time, with more money and the lessons we have learned, we can do much better. It is time to put that claim to a test in a way that will enable us to move on.

I began this chapter by saying that the educational romantics are neglecting what can be done in K–12 education. The changes below fall into that category. Money is not a problem with any of them. All of them could be done by shifting funds within existing school budgets. Technical feasibility is not a problem. Most of them would actually be easy to implement (political obstacles aside).

Find Out What Each Child's Abilities Are

If schools are to educate the students in their care, they need to know what abilities and handicaps those students bring to the classroom. In most schools, that assessment is informal or, in the better schools, limited to children who show obvious signs of problems or exceptional giftedness. There is some justification for informality. A good teacher can size up most students accurately after a few weeks. But even good teachers can make mistakes about a student's potential when dealing with children with learning disabilities or emotional problems. And not all teachers are good. Every child should receive a professional assessment of his or her palette of abilities during first grade, with periodic follow-ups to guard against diagnostic errors and to identify developmental changes. I specify "during first grade" instead of "upon entering kindergarten" to put the child at an age when cognitive measures are rapidly becoming more stable and accurate.

For the measurement of academic ability, one of the major full-scale IQ tests is appropriate. The leading options are the Woodcock-

Johnson, Wechsler, and Stanford-Binet test batteries. Each provides both an overall score and subtest scores that can yield valid and reliable fine-grained measures of the components of academic ability. Analysis of these subscores has the secondary advantage of identifying many kinds of learning disability.

The initial assessment process will cost some hundreds of dollars per child (the follow-ups, which can be selective, will be much less expensive). But we are talking about public school systems that spend on average about $11,000 per child per year. The value of obtaining a first-rate assessment of every child upon entering elementary school is worth far more than anything it will cost. The purpose is not to put students in categories etched in stone, but to give teachers a better chance to respond to their students' individual abilities and needs as they enter school and as they develop during school. Not doing such assessments now, despite the availability of the tools to do them, amounts to educational malpractice.

Give a Safe and Orderly Classroom to Every Student Who Is Trying to Learn, No Matter What

The worst inner-city schools may enroll only a small minority of the nation's children, but those schools are worse than anyone who has not been in one can imagine. They contain classes in which competent teachers cannot be heard over the din and incompetent teachers spend the class reading newspapers; classes for which the students have no textbooks; a fog of obscene language; daily student-on-student and student-on-teacher altercations, frequent assaults, periodic aggravated assaults, and the occasional aggravated assault with a deadly weapon.

There is no excuse for such schools. Buying the textbooks and identifying and getting rid of the terrible teachers is easy (technically easy, not politically easy). Getting the school under the control of the adults requires relentless enforcement of a few basic rules:

> *Disruptive students are not permitted to remain in class.* Just one student can wreck a class. A disruptive student is sent invariably and expeditiously to a holding area elsewhere.
>
> *Students who are chronically disruptive are suspended.* The meaning of *chronically* will vary from school to school, but its practical meaning is this: Suspensions are issued readily enough so that on any given day, the school has so few disruptive students in the building that the life of the school is not materially affected by them.
>
> *Students who in any way threaten a teacher verbally or physically are expelled.* Threatening a teacher attacks the core of the teacher-student relationship, and the continued presence of a student who has threatened a teacher makes the teaching environment unacceptably difficult. The student who threatens a teacher has to find another school.

Most public school systems already have rules on the books that correspond to these basics, but in many systems they are not enforced and never will be, for reasons ranging from bureaucratic pressures to political pressures to bad principals.

I should be explicit about a side effect of enforcing these simple rules in urban school systems. So many disruptive students will end up on the streets that the existing "alternative schools" cannot absorb them. The worst of the spike will be temporary—many students act out now because they know they can get away with it, and they would change their behavior if they knew they couldn't. But temporary or not, a large number of suspended and expelled students is part of the price to be paid for safe and orderly schools.

The price is not as high as it first appears. Students who are suspended are often learning nothing when they are in school—literally nothing—because they are not attending many classes, they are not paying any attention to the teacher during the classes they do attend, and they are not doing any of the homework. Nor are their hours in the school building keeping them out of trouble. The kinds of activities that get teenagers into the most trouble in the inner city (or anywhere else, for that matter) do not usually take place from 8:00 a.m. to 3:00 p.m. To say that pushing them out of the school means pushing them onto the streets is imprecise. Most of them are already on the street for all but the few hours of the day when they are preventing teachers from teaching and other students from learning.

Still, it is a price, and it can be avoided by building enough alternative schools to accommodate students ejected from regular schools. That is an issue to be decided separately. The overriding priority for inner-city schools must be the children who are trying to learn. It is morally unacceptable to continue to sacrifice their futures—and we must not kid ourselves; this is what we are doing—just because we do not know how to reach the children who are not trying to learn.

Teach the Core Knowledge Curriculum to Every Student

It is seldom that a major policy question has a completely worked-out, readily available, affordable answer. One of those rare cases is the answer to the question "What should we teach American elementary-

and middle-school students?" In chapter 3, I described the K–8 curriculum that has been developed by E. D. Hirsch's Core Knowledge Foundation. Other choices are available, notably from K^{12} Inc., which has a complete program for kindergarten through high school.

These are superb curricula, and they do not require more money or facilities to implement. They do not require exotic teaching methods or special teacher training. As a parent who has had children in both public schools and a highly regarded private school, I urge that we underestimate the strengths that the typical public school already possesses. The only thing that keeps tens of thousands of public schools from giving the average student an education competitive with that of a fine private school is the curriculum that the teachers are forced to work with. Replacements for the progressive curricula that dominate America's public schools are not only known, but are packaged and ready to use.

Let Gifted Children Go as Fast as They Can

If academically gifted children come to the end of middle school reading enthusiastically and enjoying the challenge of intellectual tasks, their test scores are irrelevant. The school has done its job. Conversely, the gifted child who reaches the end of middle school hating classes and contemptuous of the homework he is given is in big trouble. Perhaps a brilliant teacher can turn him around in later grades, or perhaps he will have a transforming experience that unleashes his potential. But the chances of that are far from certain. It is possible for academically gifted children to come out of middle school with their potential permanently crippled.

The solution is obvious and simple. Let gifted children go as fast as they can. If a third-grader is reading at the sixth-grade level, give that child sixth-grade reading. If a third-grader can do math at the sixth-grade level, give that child sixth-grade mathematics. It is a solution that should be welcomed by every reader who can remember sitting in elementary school surreptitiously reading a book while the teacher was teaching things to the rest of the class that you already knew. It also corresponds to an extensive technical literature on giftedness. Academically gifted children do well when they are given a curriculum that is complex, accelerated, and challenging, and when they have teachers with high expectations. Academically gifted children do best when they are with peers who share their interests and who do not tease them for being nerds.

Should gifted students skip grades or get advanced material within their age-appropriate grade? That's a technical issue with different answers for different children, and can be sorted out by the experts—including the child's own parents. For our purposes, two problems need to be taken seriously: wrongly leaving some children out of the accelerated education, and the stigma that special treatment of the gifted might create for everyone else.

Regarding wrong assignments: The solution is communication and openness to change. If parents feel that their child belongs in an advanced class, or the child asks to be in an advanced class, the school's first step should be to communicate to child and parents exactly what that class demands. If the parents and child still want to try, the school should agree, on this condition: Nothing in the content of the course, the way it is taught, or the way it is graded will be affected by that child's admission to the course. If he does well, then the school has corrected a placement error. If the student gets a C in the advanced course, it is up to the student to decide whether he wants to get Cs in advanced courses or go back to regular courses in which he can get As. If the student flunks, the student flunks. Such a policy pursued over time—anyone can try, but without allowances— will ensure that it must be invoked only in the uncommon cases when a genuinely questionable placement decision has been made.

Regarding stigma, these two realities about children and childhood must be recognized: First, adults do not have the option of concealing the truth. Kids know, no matter what. *When children of widely varying abilities are mixed in classes, their differences are highlighted, not obscured.* If the teacher calls on the children equally, then the deficits of the slower children are put on display for all their classmates to see. If the teacher calls only on the brighter children who know the answers, the kids quickly figure out what is going on. Children understand that academic ability varies and know the intellectual pecking order in every classroom. The slower children will get labeled whether or not they are grouped. It will be hurtful to them, to varying degrees. Educators do not have the option of preventing that hurt. What educators can do is put the relationship of performance in the classroom and merit as a person into perspective. People who are academically gifted can be fickle, humorless, dishonest, and cowardly. People who are not academically gifted can be steadfast, funny, honest, and brave. Merit as a person and academic ability are different things.

The second reality is that every child is miserable about some personal defect. It is part of being a child. The things that make children most miserable are likely to involve shortcomings in interpersonal ability—not being one of the popular kids. Many of the sources of pain come from physical appearance—having acne, being too short, being too tall, being fat, being skinny, wearing thick glasses. Poor performance in the classroom is just one of a long list of things that make children cry into their pillows at night. It is not even close to the top of the list. Performing poorly in the classroom is not a big deal socially. Performing conspicuously well is often a social liability.

I will spend no time on the argument that special treatment of the academically gifted is elitist. It has no moral standing. A special ability is a child's most precious asset. When it comes to athletic and musical ability, no one considers withholding training that could realize those gifts. It is just as senseless, and as ethically warped, to withhold training that can realize academic ability.

Teach the Forgotten Half How to Make a Living

"The forgotten half" is a term used in educational circles to refer to those who are work-bound after high school, not college-bound. If we include everyone who drops out of college or community college without a degree, that number is closer to two-thirds. The current system makes life as difficult for them as it possibly can.

First, high school has been set up so that it provides these students with no incentives to work hard. Work-bound students rightly perceive that employers of high-school graduates do not pay much attention to grades. In a large national survey, grades were said by employers to be one of the *least* important factors in hiring high-school graduates. Even if they are planning to go to a community college, students also rightly understand that most community colleges have open admissions. Economists have demonstrated with survey data what work-bound students already know. There are no short-term economic payoffs for good high-school grades. So why work hard in high school?

Then, high schools ignore the skills that employers of high-school graduates do value. Again common sense and the scholarly evidence coincide: When hiring high-school graduates, employers usually assume that they are going to have to provide the job training themselves. The purpose of the job interview is to identify young people who will show up every day and on time, work hard, and get along with the people around them. In short, they want dependability and a good attitude, and those are the qualities that the applicant had better convey during the interview.

They are qualities that schools could foster. K–12 could be thirteen years of practice for coping with the world of work. But to foster dependability and a good attitude would mean enforcing dress and language codes, and coming down hard on bad attitudes in the classroom. It would mean strict enforcement of punctuality and attendance. Few public schools think they could get away with such policies anymore, even if they tried (too much student resistance, too many parental complaints, and the danger of lawsuits). Few public school educators are even willing to say that such policies are desirable. And so after graduation many eighteen-year-olds walk into their job interviews slouching, mumbling, and dressed in ways that set off shrill alarms in the interviewer's head. They express no enthusiasm about working hard. Then they are surprised and aggrieved when they don't get hired.

Meanwhile, too many guidance counselors do not talk straight with students about their futures. Their reluctance is understandable. Counselors who try to tell students that they aren't cut out for college must be prepared for many kinds of grief—from supervisors who tell them they should be more supportive of their students' aspirations, from angry parents, and from the students themselves. But whatever the excuses, most guidance counselors now see their role as encouraging everyone to go to college—a four-year college if possible, a community college for those with the weakest academic records. Too few counselors tell work-bound high-school students how much money crane operators or stonemasons make compared to people who deliver pizza or sell shoes. Too few tell them about the new technical specialties that are being produced by a changing job market, and how much they pay. Too few assess the non-academic abilities of work-bound students and direct them toward occupations in which they can reasonably expect to succeed.

Worst of all, the current system watches these students approach the age at which they can legally drop out of school and acts as if it wants to push them out, urging them to take more mathematics, language arts, history, and science courses that they don't want to take, so that they can pursue the college chimera.

Just as public elementary schools could teach a much better curriculum with their existing facilities and staff, so also secondary schools could make education much more rewarding for work-bound students with their existing resources. Despite the current obscurity of vocational education, most school systems around the country still maintain substantial programs and facilities. The label for them is no longer vocational education, but CTE (career and technical education). The existing programs variously include classes within a comprehensive high school, special CTE schools, collaborative arrangements with the local community college, and apprenticeship programs arranged with local employers. The market is also actively engaged in providing CTE. Private postsecondary training institutes, both brick-and-mortar and online, abound.

Moreover, the empirical evidence in favor of CTE is not in

dispute. CTE works. Giving high-school students the option of tak-ing technical courses increases the likelihood they will graduate from high school. High-school students who pursue the vocational track do better in the job market, in terms of both employment rates and wages, than those who stay in the academic track but don't belong there.

In most school systems, the resources are available. They are radi-cally underused. Large numbers of students who have neither the interest nor the ability to succeed in the academic track are in it anyway, sometimes dropping out, sometimes stumbling through to the high-school diploma, never having acquired the assets that CTE could have provided. The culprit is the misbegotten, pernicious, wrong-headed idea that not going to college means you're a failure. It deforms the behavior of all the actors in America's high schools—principals, teachers, guidance counselors, students, and parents.

For practical purposes, about two-thirds of high-school students are work-bound. We should be devoting about two-thirds of our attention and resources to their needs. But the problems created by shortfalls in CTE funding and facilities are minor compared with the problem created by disdain. Choices to not attend college or to drop out of college and go to work need our understanding and—this is imperative—our respect.

Expand Choice

We have arrived at the practical question. These good things may be feasible and affordable, but how are they supposed to come to pass in the real world?

It is easy to imagine them happening in a single school. Safe and orderly schools? Disorderly schools are no fun for teachers and parents hate them. The only reason why a school is *not* safe and orderly is that forces beyond their control are preventing staff and parents from getting what both of them want. Similarly, it is easy to imagine parents and teachers agreeing that all first-graders will receive a thorough personal assessment. It is easy to imagine the principal and teachers of a school deciding to throw out the textbooks they are being given by the central system and to adopt the Core Knowledge curriculum instead (and hard to imagine many parents who would object). It is easy to imagine sixteen-year-olds asking their parents to send them to a CTE school instead of to an academic high school. It is easy to imagine guidance counselors welcoming an environment that doesn't make them push everyone toward college.

Each of the improvements I have discussed has a large constituency of receptive teachers, principals, counselors, parents, and students. Good things can happen in thousands of individual schools where parents have chosen to send their children and where the school has authority over the way it educates its students. On the other hand, none of these good things will be implemented by a large, centrally administered public school system. All of them are too politically sensitive for one reason or another. It is therefore inevitable that improvements in K–12 education will track with the success of the advocates of school choice. This is not a statement of my policy preference but of political reality. Individual schools can and will go in the directions I have just discussed if given the chance. Large school systems will dither, posture, and get nowhere.

The news about progress in school choice is mostly good. As of 2003, nearly 24,000 private elementary schools enrolled 3.6 million students. Forty states have passed laws authorizing charter schools.

The number of charter schools went from zero in 1991, when the first charter law was passed in Minnesota, to 3,294 in the 2004–2005 school year, the most recent year for which numbers are available. That number has risen substantially since then. The number of home-schooled children reached 1.1 million as of 2003, up from 850,000 only four years earlier, and it too has increased substantially since the most recent published data. Twenty years ago, the idea of tuition vouchers for low-income parents was just a gleam in a few libertarians' eyes. As of 2007, twenty-one voucher or tuition tax-credit programs were already operating, and the scope of those programs has been increasing. If we add up the parents who can afford to move to places where the public schools are to their liking, those who can afford private-school tuition, those who have access to charter schools, and those who have the option of home-schooling, some indeterminate but large proportion of American parents already enjoy a degree of school choice.

Moreover, the forces promoting school choice are gaining strength. The proportion of parents who can afford private school is increasing and will continue to increase with growth in the economy. The charter school movement, which has had to deal with the implementation problems that accompany any innovation, is going to gain momentum as the administration of charter schools improves and contrasts between ordinary public schools and the charter schools become more visible and consistent. It is not out of the question that a tipping point will occur, and that charter schools will become the modal way of administering public schools.

Home-schooling has open-ended growth potential. To home-school when a parent (usually the mother) must work out a curriculum and teach it to her children without help requires exceptional motivation and effort. But when parents can purchase an excellent curriculum off the shelf, including books, lesson plans, and lectures on DVD, home-schooling suddenly becomes easier. When it is possible to teach that curriculum with the help of classes conducted online, home-schooling gets easier still. When a few dozen other children living within driving distance are being home-schooled, one of the major disadvantages of home-schooling—the social isolation of the home-schooled child—can be neutralized. Home-schooling is getting so much easier, and is evolving so quickly, that it suggests another provocative possibility: School choice might be driven not primarily by vouchers or charter schools, but by the evolution of home-schooling into thousands of small private schools operated through a combination of parental effort, one or two professional staff members, and the exploitation of increasingly sophisticated Internet educational resources.

The school-choice movement is the most important force for good in American K–12 education. It is not wild-eyed optimism to say that the worst defects of K–12 education are going to solve themselves as the forces already in play gain momentum. As a sympathetic onlooker, I offer one piece of advice to advocates on the front lines: Stop focusing on math and reading test scores to make your case. They are the measures of educational achievement most closely tied to the child's underlying academic ability. The limits that public schools face in raising those scores also bedevil private schools, charter schools, and home-schoolers. The reason private schools, charter schools, and home-schooling are desirable is their ability to create a better education in ways that do not show up in reading and math scores.

The mostly good news about school choice is counterbalanced by one large piece of bad news. The American parents most completely shut off from choice in their children's schools are those with modest incomes who live in large cities and are forced to accept the terrible product that many urban public school systems provide. Even here, I am optimistic about the long term. The number of politicians who accept the principled arguments for school choice is growing, and they may eventually prevail. They would prevail tomorrow if they were joined by politicians who still oppose school choice for poor people but exercise it for their own children.

Use Certification to Undermine the BA

It is not inherently a problem that the four-year residential college granting a BA is inefficient and illogical. If people like it and have the money to pay for it, that's their business. The problem is that the current system creates an artificial disadvantage for the young people who don't like it, don't have the money to pay for it, or don't have the academic ability for it. That problem is complicated by the BA's function as a signal.

For those at the top of the heap, the current system provides its lucky students with a clear signal plus a halo effect. A Cornell graduate with a BA in hotel management has no problem. His prospective employer knows by the fact that he got into Cornell that he is likely to be exceptionally smart and competitive, and probably has good social skills. That he completed his BA means that he is reasonably persevering. And Cornell has the nation's most famous hotel management school.

As graduates move down the college hierarchy, the signal their

BAs send to the employer contains less information. Suppose a young woman is just as smart and persevering as the Cornell graduate, but her degree is from the University of New Hampshire. The BA now says that she went to a state university that has lots of good students, of whom she may or may not be one. Her credential still has value to the employer. The University of New Hampshire is a serious school. But just how smart and competitive she is, and how much about hotel management she really knows, is hard to tell just from knowing that she has the degree.

Now move another step down the hierarchy. This time a young man has gotten a BA in hotel management from an online school while working in low-level hotel jobs. Even if he has acquired exactly the same knowledge and skills as in the preceding two cases, the signal his BA sends now contains little useful information to the employer—perhaps less information than his job experience.

Employers are not being snobs when they give edges based on where the degree comes from. A degree from Cornell conveys information that a degree from the University of New Hampshire does not, and a degree from the University of New Hampshire conveys information that a degree from a no-name online school does not, even when the ability and knowledge of the people holding those degrees is identical. *That* is the problem, not the behavior of the employers.

To fix the problem, we need to undermine the importance of the BA. In this endeavor, we cannot expect help from many upper-middle-class parents. The current system works fine for most of their children. Nor can we expect help from politicians, who are busy advocating that more people go to college. The leverage for change comes from four realities:

- Young people entering the workforce need to be able to signal to employers what knowledge and skills they bring with them.
- Employers need to have a signal that they can interpret and trust.
- The current signal for conveying this information, the BA, is inferior—most young people and employers really do need a better one.
- A growing private postsecondary educational system is eager to help undermine the importance of the BA from brick-and-mortar four-year colleges.

The solution is not better degrees, but no degrees. Young people entering the job market should have a known, trusted measure of their qualifications that they can carry into job interviews. That measure should express what they know and are able to do, not where they learned it or how long it took them to learn it. We need certifications, not degrees.

Certifications already exist. Examples include bar exams, board certifications for medical specialties, and journeymen's tests for various crafts. For our purposes, the most applicable certification is the CPA (certified public accountant) exam. The same test is used nationwide. It is a known quantity to all employers of accountants. The test is thorough (four sections, timed, totaling fourteen hours). To achieve a passing score indicates authentic competence (the pass rate is below 50 percent for all four tests). Actual scores are reported in addition to pass/fail, so that employers can assess where the applicant falls in the distribution of accounting capability. The net result is that you can have studied accounting at an anonymous community college and be competing for a job with someone who studied it at a prestigious university, but your CPA score is what it is. If it is high, and the graduate from the prestigious university has a conspicuously lower score, suddenly prestige doesn't mean as much to an employer as it would otherwise, and neither does the anonymity of your community college. The CPA exam score does not completely eliminate the importance of the BA or of the school where it was obtained, but it goes a long way toward leveling the playing field.

The merits of the CPA exam apply to any college major for which the BA is now used as a job qualification. To name just some of them: journalism, criminal justice, social work, public administration, and the many separate majors under the headings of business, computer science, engineering, engineering technology, and education. Such majors accounted for almost two-thirds of bachelor's degrees conferred in 2005.

CPA-like certification tests have the least leveling effect for professions requiring advanced degrees. Holding a law degree from Harvard remains an advantage independently of a job applicant's score on the bar exam. But for professions that do not require an advanced degree, the availability of a nationally recognized certification test could often turn the current evaluations of applicants upside down. Return to our three BAs in hotel management. Without a certification exam, the Cornell graduate has an edge and the online graduate is at the bottom. Show the employer identical test scores on a demanding hotel management exam, and suddenly the balance flips. Who has achieved that score against tougher odds? Who has already demonstrated more commitment to a career in hotel management? It is the Cornell graduate who is on the defensive in these comparisons, not the online student.

So far I have referred to occupations that commonly require a BA as a ticket to a job interview, but certification tests also apply across the whole range of technical occupations that are now mostly taught at community colleges. In fact, it is hard to think of an occupation for which a good certification test would not be more useful than the ambiguous signal sent by the degree, whether that degree be a BA, AA, or high-school diploma.

Certification tests will not reduce the importance of academic ability. Even though the items in the tests are tightly focused on the practical content of the occupation in question, people with high linguistic and logical-mathematical ability will still have an edge. That's why those abilities are so valuable—they are all-purpose tools for getting ahead in life. Graduates of prestigious colleges will have higher certification scores on average than people who have taken online courses, just because prestigious colleges attract academically talented people. But that's irrelevant to the larger issue. Under a certification system, four years is not required, residence is not required, expensive tuitions are not required, and a degree is not required. Equal educational opportunity means, among other things, creating a society in which it's what you know that makes the difference. Substituting certification for degrees would be a big step in the right direction. And the incentives are right. Almost everyone benefits.

The most obvious beneficiaries are all employers and all young people who are not attending well-known traditional colleges. Certification provides the employers with valuable and trustworthy new information about applicants at no cost. It offers the students a new resource for competing with their luckier peers.

Certification tests also benefit the large postsecondary educational industry that has grown up outside the system of brick-and-mortar four-year colleges. Online schools know that the BAs they award do not have the gravitas of a BA from a traditional four-year college. Nationally recognized certification tests get them out from under that disadvantage. Online schools can credibly promise that students with a given level of academic ability can get certification scores that are competitive with those of students of the same ability attending traditional colleges, and do it far more quickly and cheaply.

The only people who do not benefit from certification tests are students at well-known traditional colleges. For high-achieving students at those schools, certification tests are a wash. They lose some of the halo effect of going to a good school, but that is offset by whatever real advantage the college offers in the quality of its education, which will be reflected in their test scores.

Certification tests hurt just one set of people: students who have gotten into prestigious schools, who under the current system benefit from a halo effect that goes with a BA from those schools, but who are actually coasting through their courses and would score poorly on a certification test. This is an outcome devoutly to be wished.

No technical barriers stand in the way of certification tests. Hundreds of such tests already exist. The problem is not lack of tests, but lack of tests that are nationally recognized in the way that the SAT and ACT are nationally recognized for use in college admissions. Fortunately, markets tend to fill needs if they can be filled at a profit. In this instance, the first step is to articulate the role that certification tests could serve and start people talking about the advantages they would reap. Once enough people are talking about them, a high-profile testing company such as the Educational Testing Service needs to make a strategic decision to create definitive certification tests, coordinating with major employers, professional groups, and nontraditional universities to make their creations the gold standard.

In an environment in which so many actors would benefit from having nationally recognized certification standards, it can be done.

At the end of the process lies the ideal system that I envision. Community colleges and four-year campuses still look the way they used to, but the way that students use those facilities has changed. Fewer students are trying to use community college as a stepping-stone to a four-year college, because the BA no longer is their goal. These students don't take courses just so their transcript shows the prerequisites required for the four-year college application. They focus on a vocational specialty instead.

In traditional colleges, students who are aiming for law, medicine, or a PhD are still enrolled in a four-year curriculum leading to a BA. The best professional and graduate schools still want their applicants to have four years of pre-med, pre-law, and liberal arts courses under their belts. Some students are staying for four years just because college life is fun and their parents are paying for it. A few old-fashioned students are there for four years and a BA because they want a liberal education. But most of the other students in traditional colleges are there for the amount of time it takes them to learn the vocation they want to learn.

Usually, taking the courses they need will consume just two or three years. But some of these vocationally oriented students will be staying for four years because they are taking more advanced undergraduate courses in their specialty than they used to. When the destination was the BA, students had little incentive to take more courses than their major required. When the destination is a comprehensive certification test, and advanced courses can raise that score, taking additional courses makes sense. Students graduating after four years typically have finished a course load that used to indicate an MA in their specialty.

Another healthy change is that more students in vocationally oriented colleges discover during their college experience that they enjoy learning. They are working harder in their courses than their counterparts under the old system because they actually need to learn the material if they want a high certification score—getting a B for the transcript is no longer enough. In the process of working hard, some students discover they're good at learning and enjoy exercising that realized capacity. Once that happens, the gates open to other possibilities.

Sometimes, the student who has discovered he enjoys college-level work will start expanding his course interests. Since he doesn't want a BA, he won't be trying to figure out the easiest course that will fulfill the humanities requirement. If he decides to take a course outside his vocational interest, it will be because he wants to take it. Sometimes it will be a course on television sitcoms, and nothing will come of it. But undergraduates who have discovered that they enjoy intellectual challenges will sometimes enroll in a course on Renaissance art or on the English novel. Once they do that, and enjoy it, lives can be transformed.

Often, the rewards will come after college. A person who has discovered that he enjoys the challenge of difficult books is a person who, years later, is open to picking up a biography of George Marshall at the bookstore and becoming a World War II expert, or a person who decides to give *War and Peace* a try and ends up reading the whole Tolstoy corpus. As evidence that this happens, I appeal to readers: How many of the avocations that have absorbed you as an adult, and in which you have become quite knowledgeable, have anything to do with the content of a course you took in college?

In my ideal system, changes in technology have altered the college experience in other ways that no one could have foreseen, and so

I can hardly describe them now. But they all tend in the direction of more flexibility, more options, more competition among the providers of education, and lower costs to the student.

The greatest merit of my ideal system is this: Hardly any jobs still have the BA as a requirement for a fair shot at being hired. Employers are relying more on direct evidence about what the job candidate knows, less on where or how it was learned. The world isn't perfect, but opportunities are wider and fairer, and the stigma of not having a BA diminishes with every additional person who obviously has the academic ability to get a BA but who no longer bothers to do so.

The Challenge: Liberal Education Redux

I have left the most vexing problem for last. Nothing in any of the other reforms I have proposed does anything to remedy the defects in the postsecondary education of the gifted that I discussed in chapter 4. A large proportion of the academically gifted students who will run the country in the next generation would still be reaching the end of their long educational careers ignorant in some of the most important ways—sloppy in their verbal expression, unschooled in tools that they will need to make good decisions, innocent of any systematic thought about the meaning of a human life, oblivious to all of these shortcomings in their education, and oblivious to their own intellectual limits.

In looking for solutions, parents should have a role to play, but, realistically, they won't play it. When it comes to shopping for colleges, many parents of America's brightest students—disproportionately affluent and well-educated themselves—act like drugged-up pop stars on Rodeo Drive. They buy by brand name without checking quality, pay huge premiums without getting value in return, and, once they've ordered the product, don't follow up to see whether the seller delivered. I see no prospects that this kind of parental behavior will change. As the number of affluent parents increases, the competition among them to get their children into prestigious colleges will become even more frantic. Harvard and Stanford could probably triple (quadruple? quintuple?) their tuitions and still have more applicants than they could admit.

I could present compelling empirical evidence that this obsession about getting one's child into a prestigious college is irrational, but it would be pointless. As long as they aren't making any more coastline, the price of beachfront property will go up, and as long as they aren't making any more prestigious colleges, the competition to get into them will increase. Aside from that, there's the indulgence factor to consider. Even parents who realize that paying Idyllic College $40,000 a year doesn't buy a better undergraduate education than their child could get at State U., and who realize that the connections that come with an Idyllic College degree aren't really that important, will fork over the tuition money if their child has his heart set on going to Idyllic College. Combine the parents who are buying education heedlessly and those who are buying indulgently, and we do not have consumers who inspire sellers to improve their product.

We can expect no help from today's faculties. For every scholar who pleads for colleges to return to their historic mission, a half dozen are disdainful of Canons, dismissive of Dead White Males and committed to seeing the humanities through the prism of race, class, and gender. For every faculty member who is ready to give Cs for pedestrian work, a half dozen do not want the hassle that tough grading brings.

We can expect no help from college administrators. Presidents and deans of private colleges want to attract as many applicants as possible. A surefire way to drive down applications is to require an extensive and demanding core curriculum. Witness the retreat of an institution as august as the University of Chicago, which a few years ago gutted its famous core requirements.

We can expect no help from the gifted students themselves. Eighteen-year-olds put in front of a smorgasbord of enticing courses are not adept decision-makers even if they are motivated to challenge themselves. Those who are not motivated to challenge themselves make even worse decisions.

And so, unlike the changes in education that I have advocated up to this point, we cannot rely upon the natural inclinations and interests of parents, students, or employers to push change in the right direction if given a chance. In the case of college and the gifted student, a change in mind-set must come first.

We have four things working in favor of such a change. First, the stuff of a liberal education is truly wonderful. At scattered moments and places in the course of human history, *Homo sapiens* has created works that speak to the human condition with depth and insight that place them qualitatively apart. The works in the pantheon are not just from the West. Much from outside the West should be incorporated into the curriculum of a liberal education, not to fill out a multicultural checklist but because the work is authentically worthy. But a consensus exists about a core of great work that must be part of a liberal education. Among those who understand their fields the best, no one denies that Plato, Aristotle, Kant, Beethoven, Mozart, Bach, Michelangelo, Da Vinci, Rembrandt, Shakespeare, Homer, and a few dozen others are indispensable. Their specific places in the pantheon may be argued, and the arguments about who is essential and who is peripheral increase as the list is expanded, but it comes down to this: A college can keep any undergraduate busy for four years without coming close to exhausting the body of work that is great beyond dispute.

The second thing we have going for us is that professors are deeply motivated to show their peers how smart they are—exhibiting smartness is the only way to score points that count in academia. The way to do that is to say smart things about difficult problems in their fields. For the last few decades, intellectual fashion has made it possible for professors to score points by being tricky-smart. The postmodernists in literary criticism are an excellent example, using impenetrable vocabulary to make convoluted arguments in proof of points of a triviality and sophistry that would excite the envy of a medieval theologian. It works for a while, but only for a while. Ultimately, for a literature professor to be smart about Molière or Yeats requires insights into what the author was talking about. Similarly, philosophy professors can take logical positivism only so far; ultimately, they have to be smart about the great issues of metaphysics and ethics, which means being smart about Descartes and Spinoza. Scholars of the fine arts can take a Piss Christ and installation art only so far; ultimately, they have to be smart about Dürer and Velázquez. I cannot predict how long it will take, but the greatest work must ultimately come back into scholarly fashion.

The third thing we have going for us is that the questions a liberal education addresses are questions that students cannot help asking themselves. The meaning of life is on the mind of just about every college sophomore. The more acute the student's intellectual awareness, the closer to the front of the mind such questions are likely to be. Many of these students think they have to find answers *de novo*. It has never occurred to them that the meaning of life is a topic that can be explored systematically. Getting them to enroll in Philosophy 101 or to read *King Lear* is sometimes as simple as letting them know that the giants of the past can help them think about things that they already want to think about.

The fourth and perhaps ultimately the most effective force that can lead to better education of the gifted is the truth of Aristotle's insight: One of the deepest forms of human enjoyment is the exercise of one's realized capacities. Gifted students who think it is fun to get by with less than their best are wrong. It is not nearly as much fun as becoming really, really good at something. To do that, it is almost always necessary to have someone beckoning, guiding, and pushing. That's what great teachers, and great colleges, are for. The attraction to excellence is not a pious expression of what gifted children should feel, but a truth about what most gifted children will feel if the environment does not prevent them.

These are reasons for long-term optimism, not short-term expectations. It will take some time before the mind-set changes. Writing about the problem is the contribution that is within my grasp.

Taking Responsibility

There is no shortage of blame to parcel out for the unreality of today's educational system. The politicians and the education establishment bear much of the blame for the problems of elementary and secondary education. Parents bear much of the blame for the problems of postsecondary education. When it comes to the reality of varying abilities and their implications, we have all been complicit in turning a blind eye.

If there is to be a return to reality, it will not come from government. Of all the people hooked on wishful thinking, politicians have the most untreatable habit. A return to reality will happen through the decisions of parents who can make choices about the schooling of their children, and eventually, through the recognition that all parents should be able to make such choices. It will come through the recognition by educators that most of the teenagers in their charge want and need to learn to make a living. It will come through employers asking for evidence of what their applicants know instead of using the BA as a screening device. It will come through parents and professors who demand that the gifted be worthy of their good luck.

Above all, it will come through a resumption of responsibility by the grown-ups. There is no argument about the ultimate goal of education. It is expressed just right by the Army's old recruiting slogan "Be All That You Can Be." That's what education should help each child to do. But that slogan has a snare: the word *can*. It is not good enough just to wish children well. It is our obligation as adults to oversee their journey. Sometimes that means encouraging, reinforcing, and praising—things that make us feel good. But dealing with *can* imposes less pleasant roles as well. When the child's potential is unlimited, making good on our obligation sometimes means pushing, criticizing, and demanding—things that make us feel like the bad guy. When a child's aspirations really are unrealistic, making good on our obligation means guiding the child toward other goals— something else that makes us feel like the bad guy. But part of being a grown-up is accepting that role when necessary. Parents and educators alike have blinked at that reality for decades now. It is our children who have paid the price.

That is the sobering part of the Army slogan. The other part is about opening up possibilities. Parents and educators alike should be rooting for children to shoot for the stars—and telling them to find their own. It is a tough sell. Our culture exalts the advanced degree and the big office and the big salary. But it is within our power to tell our children differently, and to be telling them the absolute truth. *They will have succeeded if they discover something they love doing and learn how to do it well.* To say that this accomplishment is more important than making a lot of money and more important than fame or prestige is not idealism. For those of us who have been lucky enough to be happy in our adult vocations or avocations, it is the reality of our lives.

Educational success needs to be redefined accordingly. The goal of education is to bring children into adulthood having discovered things they enjoy doing and doing them at the outermost limits of their potential. The goal applies equally to every child, across the entire range of every ability. There are no first-class and second-class ways to enjoy the exercise of our realized capacities. It is a quintessentially *human* satisfaction, and its universality can connect us all. Opening the door to that satisfaction is what real education does.

Notes

These notes are intended to help readers who want to pursue topics that interest them, not to give the level of documentation that is appropriate to a journal article. The best way to achieve that goal is to use sources that you can find easily—preferably online—and to give a single source that reviews the state of knowledge on a topic rather than to list a dozen separate journal articles.

Many of the education statistics come from the website of the National Center for Education Statistics (NCES). Rather than repeat the URLs many times, here are the two main ones: For *The Digest of Education Statistics 2006*, http://nces.ed.gov/programs/digest/, and for the many reports about the National Assessment of Educational Progress, http://nces.ed.gov/nationsreportcard/. All of the NCES statistics cited in the text can be found online. All the URLs were accessed between May 2007 and February 2008.

To learn more about the main topics of *Real Education*, a few books are central. For all the fraught questions involving abilities and intelligence, read Howard Gardner's *Frames of Mind* and Arthur Jensen's *The g Factor*, and you will know everything you need to know. And then some. Three other key books are E. D. Hirsch's *Cultural Literacy* on K–8 education, James Rosenbaum's *Beyond College for All* on the education of those for whom college is not right, and

Anthony Kronman's *Education's End* on the role of liberal education at the college level.

My policy is to give a specific page reference for all direct quotes. When I make a general statement about a source's findings, I usually just give the source, or the chapter within a book-length source. There are a few lengthy narrative notes on points that seemed especially important, but for the most part I exercised restraint. I omitted footnote numbers in the text to avoid cluttering a conversational presentation.

A style note about the main text: As always, I adhere to the Murray Rule for dealing with third-person singular pronouns, which prescribes using the gender of the author or principal author as the default, and I hope in vain that others will adopt it.

Chapter 1

17 The initial book-length presentation of multiple intelligences was Howard Gardner's *Frames of Mind* (Gardner, 1983), from which the descriptions of the seven intelligences are abstracted. Newer editions are in print.

22 Data on occupations are taken from the Bureau of Labor Statistics website at http://www.bls.gov/oes/oes_dl.htm.

23–4 The seminal article on *g* is Spearman (1904). The encyclopedic source is still Arthur Jensen's *The* g *Factor* (Jensen, 1998), though much has happened since it was published, especially in neuroscience, which has found that *g* correlates both with the size of specific regions of the brain and with a variety of physiological responses. See, for example, Haier, Jung, Yeo, Head, and Alkire (2004), Colom, Jung, and Haier (2006), and Thompson et al. (2001). If you insist on getting your information on *g* from

Stephen J. Gould's best-selling *Mismeasure of Man* (Gould, 1981), you should at least read the scientific community's assessment of it, as in Carroll (1995).

25 For the interrelationship of linguistic, spatial, and logical-mathematical ability to g, see Jensen (1998), chapters 2 to 4, and Matarazzo (1972), chapter 11.

26 On the interpretation of SAT scores, it must be remembered that the SAT scores reported in the newspapers every year refer to the latest results for the subset of seventeen-year-olds who are not only trying to get into college, but trying to get into colleges that require the SAT. They are a self-selected group with academic ability far above the national average. See chapter 3 and its notes for a discussion of the SAT scores that would be obtained if all seventeen-year-olds took the test.

26 On whether to use an aggregated measure such as an IQ score or disaggregated subscores, there are some instances when subscores are important even with large samples. For example, knowing the combined SAT-Math and SAT-Verbal scores among exceptionally gifted young people who took the SAT at age thirteen is important in explaining their level of creative accomplishment thirty-five years later, but knowing the difference between the SAT-Math and SAT-Verbal scores is important in explaining the type of careers in which those accomplishments occurred (Park, Lubinski, and Benbow, 2007).

26–7 The statistical relationships between IQ and the various personality relationships were taken from Ackerman and Heggestad (1997), Judge, Bono, Ilies, and Gerhardt (2002), Judge, Colbert, and Ilies (2004), and Reeve, Meyer, and Bonaccio (2006). For readers who are wondering why I do not employ measures of emotional intelligence (EI), made famous by Daniel Goleman's best-selling book *Emotional Intelligence* (Goleman, 1995), the answer is that the proponents of EI are still on the defensive in making the case that EI hangs together as a construct or that measures of it add anything to existing personality measures. For a dialogue between defenders and critics, see Mayer, Salovey, and Caruso (2004) and the commentaries that follow it. The most comprehensive analysis of emotional intelligence as a construct and of the attempts to operationalize it is Matthews, Zeidner, and Roberts (2004). Another major source is Geher (2004).

28 For the relationship of musical ability to IQ, Shuter (1968) has a literature review of sixty-five studies. Subsequent work includes Lynn and Gault (1986), and Good, Aggleton, Kentridge, Barker, and Neave (1997).

Chapter 2

33–4 For checking out your local schools, try www.schoolmatters.com and www.greatschools.net/. You can also check the website for your state's department of education. To estimate underrepresentation of below-average academic ability in affluent suburbs, I used data from www.mdreportcard.org for a sampling of schools to calculate the skew in affluent Maryland suburbs. If you want to replicate the exercise for your local school, here's how:

The preferred method is to use the test score mean and standard deviation for the state (M_S and SD_S) and the mean score for your local school (M_L). You can compute the standard score of the average student in your school relative to the statewide population of students (Z_L) using the equation $Z_L = (M_L - M_S)/SD_S$. To find the percentile this standard score represents in a normally distributed set of test scores, use a table of cumulative probabilities for a normal distribution or (this way is a lot easier) enter the standard score into the function NORMSDIST in Microsoft Excel or the equivalent formula in another software package. Suppose that NORMSDIST yields .75 as the result. In that case, the average student in your school is at the 75th percentile of all students in the state.

Many states and local schools do not report means and standard deviations, instead giving only the percentages passing the Basic, Proficient, and Advanced levels of the test. In this case, you can still estimate where your school stands. To illustrate how, suppose that you have the percentage passing the Advanced reading level in your school (P_L) and in your state (P_S). Enter those numbers expressed as proportions (e.g., enter 75 percent as .75) into the formula "= NORMSINV(P_L) − NORMSINV(P_S)" in Microsoft Excel, or its equivalent in another software package. This will give you an estimate of the difference between your school and the state average in terms of standard deviations. To improve the estimate, also calculate the estimate for those meeting the Proficient level in reading, and the comparable estimates for the math test, and take the median or mean of all the estimates. Enter this result into NORMSDIST, and you once again will have the percentile score for your school relative to the state average. It will not be as accurate as the percentile based on the actual means and standard deviations, but will be usably close. For a full description of this method of estimating group differences and its application to various topics, see http://www.lagriffedulion.f2s.com/.

35 For more examples of NAEP test questions, go to http://nces.ed.gov/nationsreportcard/itmrls/, where you can also retrieve the test materials for the examples in the text.

36 The calculation of wrong answers does not include students who omitted the item. On the calculation of the students who got the right answer by guessing, the procedure in the text assumes that someone who does not know the answer to an item is equally likely to choose any of the x alternatives. With complete psychometric information about response patterns, about people who did not answer the item at all versus those who chose an alternative, and other information, a more precise estimate could be made.

43 The quotation from Thorndike's 1917 article, "Reading as reasoning," is taken from Jensen (1998): 281.

43 On the questions about Roosevelt and the Bill of Rights, the data can be found at the NAEP site given above. Forty-one percent missed the Roosevelt question and about another 14 percent got the right answer by guessing. Forty-eight percent missed the Bill of Rights question and about 16 percent got the right answer by guessing.

48 On the relationship of IQ scores to academic achievement, the number of articles on the subject comes from Jensen (1998): 277, who also reviews the findings of that literature, along with the literature on attempts to find some independent measure of learning ability, in chapter 9. For a more recent review of the literature along with the results from an excellent British database, see Deary, Strand, Smith, and Fernandes (2007). For a recent article dealing with a common objection—that education predicts IQ scores rather than the other way around—see Watkins, Lei, and Canivez (2007).

50 On the effects of adoption, the definitive literature review is
   Locurto (1990). It is harder than one would expect to find evidence that abuse in the home lowers IQ scores independently of
   the mother's IQ, but I take it as given that such extreme behaviors as locking children in a closet for long periods of time, or
   never talking to them, has an effect. For evidence on the causal
   relationship between environmental disadvantages such as
   poverty and cognitive skills, McLoyd (1998) offers a good review.
   On neuroplasticity, an entertaining popular account is Doidge
   (2007). For recent findings about the effects of high stress
   during infancy and early childhood on brain development,
   see Irvine (2004), retrieved from http://www.sciencedaily.com/
   releases/2004/10/041021082832.htm.

50 On the effects of a change of three points in a population's mean
   IQ, see Herrnstein and Murray (1994): 364–68. It is the effect of
   small changes on large populations that drives the arguments for
   the cost-effectiveness of preschool interventions. For a synthesis
   of that evidence, see Heckman and Masterov (2007). Arthur
   Jensen recalls making the statement about not paying five cents
   to raise his IQ five points (Jensen, 2008, personal communication), but neither he nor I can find a published source.

51–4 For reviews of attempts to raise intelligence, see Jensen (1998):
   333–44, Spitz (1986), and Herrnstein and Murray (1994):
   393–410. Sternberg (1995) argues that Herrnstein and I were too
   pessimistic. Spitz (2001) refutes Sternberg's position point by
   point. The review of studies conducted by the Consortium is
   found in Lazar and Darlington (1982). The quotation in the text
   comes from page 47.

   On the Abecedarian Project, the literature is large and

disputatious, probably inevitably because of two built-in problems: The experimental and control samples were so small that
the results are vulnerable to statistical anomalies, and the people
who conducted the Abecedarian Project also had complete control over the evaluation and its data from the beginning to the
most recent publications. This is not a commentary on the specific people involved, but on a structural problem that affects
many demonstration programs (Perry Preschool is another
famous example). People who conduct intensive interventions for
disadvantaged children are not disinterested observers. Simple
honesty is not the issue. In the law, it is taken for granted that
nobody may ever be allowed to be judge in his own case. The reasons for that principle apply equally to the evaluations of experimental programs. The data regarding early and late results of the
Abecedarian Project come from Spitz (1992) and Campbell, Pungello, Miller-Johnson, Burchinal, and Ramey (2001): Table 1,
respectively.

On the results for the IHDP, the two tests of cognitive ability
were the Peabody Picture Vocabulary Test and the Wechsler
Abbreviated Scale of Intelligence. The numbers in the text are
based on the marginal mean scores corrected for sample attrition.
The statement about the nearly identical scores is based on the
combined results for all subjects in the study, which I calculated
from the data in McCormick, Brooks-Gunn, Buka, et al. (2006),
Tables 3 and 4. Combining the data follows the precedent set by
evaluators of the IHDP in its first follow-up, when the children
were tested at two and three years of age and the experimental
group showed large gains across the board (Brooks-Gunn, Liaw,
and Klebanov, 1992). In the second follow-up at age five, when

those gains for the total sample had disappeared, Brooks-Gunn et al. (1994) reported statistics for the total sample and for two subgroups with birth weights above and below 2,000 grams. The comparable tables for the follow-up at age eighteen in McCormick, Brooks-Gunn, Buka et al. (2006) did not present the results for the combined sample, instead showing only the breakdown for the two weight groups.

Which of these two groups, the lighter or heavier LBW babies, was of greater interest to the researchers when the study began? The authors of Brooks-Gunn et al. (1992) wrote that "Because lighter LBW preterm infants are more likely to have developmental problems, two-thirds of the children were in the lighter LBW group. We included heavier LBW preterm infants because they are at risk for delays and because this type of intervention had not been used with either group of LBW preterm infants." Another article about the early results, McCormick, McCarton, Tonascia, and Brooks-Gunn (1993), described the project's purpose this way: "OBJECTIVE: To examine the effect of early educational intervention after discharge from the hospital on the health and developmental status of very low birth weight ($\leq$ 1,500 gm) infants." The article was entirely devoted to the positive results for babies weighing less than 1,500 grams.

At the end of it all, the group that warranted two-thirds of the study's resources did slightly worse than the controls. The results for all of the subjects combined were effectively identical for the tests of intellectual ability, academic achievement, behavioral problems, and physical health—exactly the results one would expect from a well-executed randomized design for a program that had no effect. And yet here is the conclusion the authors of

McCormick et al. (2006) reached: "[T]his phase of the IHDP provides important support for the efficacy of early educational intervention in the longer-term outcomes of children." (778) This example shows why you must never read just the final paragraphs of a technical article about the evaluation of a social program. The conclusions are often rosier than a detached view of the data might suggest. For a full-blown technical debate over the IHDP results, see Baumeister and Bacharach (2000) and Blair and Whalsten (2002).

52 On the meaning and uses of the standard deviation, a description may be found in Appendix 1 of Herrnstein and Murray (1994). The example of the different widths of percentiles using SAT scores is based on a mean of 500 and a standard deviation of 100, the scale to which the SAT was recentered in 1995.

56 On educational levels prevailing at the beginning of the twentieth century, see Stedman and Kaestle (1991): 127. Enrollment rates are taken from Table 7 in the *Digest of Education Statistics 2006*.

56–7 On the Long-Term Trend Assessment, it must be understood that NAEP consists of two separate sets of tests. The one you read about in the newspapers every time its results are published is called the Main NAEP Assessment. Another, shorter test remained essentially unchanged from the first administrations of NAEP in the early 1970s until 2004. This is the Long-Term Trend Assessment, and it provides the most accurate measure of changes over time. More information on the two tests and their differences can be found at NAEP's website. Readers who want to explore the data for themselves can download the Long-Term Trend Assessment from http://nces.ed .gov/nationsreportcard/ltt/results2004/. The relevant graphs are figures 2-1 and 2-2 on pages 10–12 and 2-4 and 2-5 on pages 17–20.

Interpreting the Long-Term Trend Assessment scores from the 1970s and early 1980s is complicated because improvements probably reflect a recovery from a decline that started in the mid-1960s. It is a murky picture. The best-known evidence for the decline is SAT scores, but they reflect the subset of students who take the SAT and their interpretation is complicated by a changing pool of test-takers. The SAT decline began in 1964 and bottomed out in 1981. The SAT-Verbal and the SAT-Math have never returned to their means of the early 1960s. The Iowa Test of Basic Skills, administered to all Iowa students, shows a steep decline in both verbal and mathematics tests beginning in 1965 and bottoming out in 1979, but scores on both tests had recovered to their pre-decline highs by 1984. The SAT norm studies conducted in 1955, 1960, 1966, 1974, and 1983, using nationally representative samples of all high-school students, show no evidence of a decline. Scores in 1960 and 1983 were almost identical. For details on this complicated story, see Herrnstein and Murray (1994): 421–25. For our purposes, the salient point is that no test data indicate that reading and math test scores among elementary and secondary students were higher at the beginning of the 1980s than they had been at the beginning of the 1960s, hence the need for caution in interpreting improvements in the 1970s as representing new heights.

57 The discussion of the math required by NAEP is drawn from Loveless (2004) and Loveless (2007). The direct quote in the text comes from page 6 of Loveless (2007). In many respects, the reading test tries to do the same thing with its many items involving

reading in context (e.g., examples 5 and 6 in the text of chapter 2). It would be useful to know whether the gains in reading scores among low-ability students were concentrated in such items, but I have not found such an analysis.

58–9 On the Coleman report, the original version is Coleman et al. (1966). The reports of the reanalyses are given in Mosteller and Moynihan (1972). Ironically, the only finding of the Coleman Report that did not hold up under further analysis was the conclusion that integrated classrooms promoted higher achievement among black students—and that was the one finding actually applied to policy. The Coleman Report was cited on behalf of widespread school busing from the late 1960s into the late 1970s.

59–60 On Title I and its evaluations over the years, an excellent review, along with original analyses bearing on the 1990s, is Kosters and Mast (2003). It may be downloaded from the American Enterprise Institute website, www.aei.org. The data on the growing gap between high-poverty and low-poverty schools are taken from Figures 1-3 and 1-4.

59 On the relationship of parental income and the child's IQ, the correlation is about +.4, meaning that low academic ability is heavily skewed toward low-income families. In the best nationally representative sample with information on parental income, for example, 75 percent of children in the bottom quintile of parental income were in the lower half of the distribution on the measure of IQ. Among children in the top quintile of parental income, only 24 percent were in the lower half. These figures were prepared by the author using the 1979 cohort of the National Longitudinal Survey of Youth, hereafter designated as the NLSY-79. A description of

the survey and its cognitive measure, the Armed Forces Qualification Test, can be found in Appendix 2 and Appendix 3 in Herrnstein and Murray (1994).

61 On NCLB's effects on test scores, I do not report results from the
state-level exams. Some of them make much more optimistic
claims than NAEP results show, but assessing the validity of
those claims is keeping a small army of psychometricians busy.
For discussions of the many ways in which high-stakes testing
produces inflated and sometimes bogus results, see Koretz (2007)
and Herman and Haertel (2005). A good analysis of results up to
2006 is Lee (2006).

62 On inner-city schools, many descriptions are available. Jonathan
Kozol has been writing such accounts since *Death at an Early Age*
forty years ago (Kozol, 1967). Other accounts include Stern
(2003), Noguera (2003), and Anyon (1997). An excellent
unadorned account of day-to-day life in an inner-city school is
Lonnae Parker's recent series on Coolidge High for the *Washington Post*, available online at the *Washington Post* website for a fee
(Parker, 2007a, 2007b, 2007c). The data on students attending
schools in large cities were obtained from the *Digest of Education
Statistics 2006*, Table 86.

63 On the description of NAEP's Basic reading level for eighth-
graders, see http://nces.ed.gov/nationsreportcard/reading/
achieveall.asp. On the absence of information about the joint
distribution of IQ and NAEP scores, it is hard to believe that no one
has ever done this obvious analysis. I have searched a variety of bib-
liographic databases and made inquiries of the National Center for
Education Statistics without turning up any relevant work. Perhaps
my claim that none exists will unearth something.

65 On vouchers, my advocacy goes back to the concluding chapter of
   Losing Ground (Murray, 1984). See also Murray (1988), chapters
   10 and 11, and Murray (1997): 90–97. I remain nervous about the
   degree of regulation that the government would impose on private education if a voucher program were enacted.

   The empirical literature bearing on the potential effects of
   school-choice programs began in 1982 with the publication of
   High School Achievement: Public, Catholic, and Private Schools, coau-
   thored by James Coleman of the Coleman Report (Coleman, Hoffer, and Kilgore, 1982). In the 1990s, that literature began to be
   augmented by the evaluations of pilot voucher programs, notably
   in Milwaukee, and then by evaluations of charter schools. For an
   excellent recent summary of the findings and an extensive bibli-
   ography, see Walberg (2007).

   The technical difficulties in drawing comparisons between
   children who get vouchers and those who do not are formidable
   because of self-selection effects. As I write, there have been five
   random assignment voucher experiments that mitigate that
   problem. In Charlotte, North Carolina, the experimental group
   showed net gains (all of the following results refer to comparisons with the control group) of 4 to 6 percentile points in math
   and 5 to 8 percentile points in reading after one year (Greene,
   2001 and Cowen, 2007). In Dayton, the black members of the
   experimental group showed a 6.5-percentile-point gain overall
   after two years but not whites (Howell and Peterson, 2006). In
   Milwaukee, one study found a 6-percentile-point gain in reading
   and an 11-percentile-point gain in math after four years (Greene,
   Peterson, and Du, 1999), but another that included more extensive controls (Rouse, 1998) found a positive effect only for math

(about 8 percentile points after four years). In Washington, a privately funded voucher experiment produced a 9-percentile-point gain for African-American students after two years (Howell and Peterson, 2006). The subsequent publicly funded DC Opportunity Scholarship Program did not find a statistically significant impact after one year (Wolf et al., 2007). If you want to see just how technically complex these assessments become, go to http://biosun01.biostat.jhsph.edu/~cfrangak/papers/sc/vouchers.pdf, where you will find an article, three comments on it, and rejoinder about the New York City voucher experiment. The target article, Barnard, Frangakis, Hill, and Rubin (2003), found that experimental subjects from low-achieving schools achieved a 3- to 5-percentile-point gain on math scores that reached statistical significance. A reanalysis of the data in one of the comments, Kreuger and Zhu (2003), found smaller changes that did not reach statistical significance. None of these evaluations in any of the experimental sites as yet have data on the fadeout effects that have been universally observed in attempts to raise IQ.

Chapter 3

68 The number of bachelor's degrees in 2005 comes from *Digest of Educational Statistics 2006*, Table 257. The number of twenty-three-year-olds comes from Bureau of the Census population projections, available at http://www.census.gov/population/www/projections/popproj.html.

68 For alternative measures of college readiness and their calculation, see Kobrin (2007), which is also the source for the discussion of the College Board's college readiness benchmarks. On 115 as the modal IQ for college around mid-century see, for example,

Matarazzo (1972), pages 178–179. For changes across time and differences among colleges, see Herrnstein and Murray (1994), chapter 1. For the percentage of adults with a BA, see *Digest of Education Statistics 2006*, Table 8.

69 The benchmark for the combined score does not equal the total of the benchmarks for the SAT-Verbal and SAT-Math separately because, put roughly, fewer people get high scores on both of two separate tests than get a high score on one of two tests.

70 The estimate of how many American seventeen-year-olds meet the benchmark scores was reached using three independent methods that yield parallel results.

Method I. The first method starts with the fact that a combined score of 1180 or higher was achieved by the top 25 percent of students who took the SAT in 2005 (Kobrin, 2007). Those who take the SAT are a self-selected population with academic ability well above the national average. In 2005, they constituted about 47 percent of high-school graduates that year and 35 percent of all seventeen-year-olds. How many of the 65 percent who do *not* take the SAT could get 1180 or higher? Suppose we establish a lower bound, assuming that none of those who did not take the SAT would have gotten a combined score of 1180 or higher (an underestimate). In that case, the 1180 benchmark would have included only 8.8 percent of seventeen-year-olds in 1995. The upper bound cannot be a large proportion. Students with high enough academic promise to get an 1180 on the SAT typically apply to several schools, one of which requires the SAT, even in the Midwest and South, where the ACT is most widely used. Applications for scholarships and other awards typically require SAT scores. Counselors who see high-school students with high academic

promise urge them to take the SAT. I will use an upper-bound estimate of 4 percent. To see how implausibly high this is, think in
terms of an average public high school with a graduating class of
500 students in 2005. Forty-seven percent of them (235) took the
SAT, and 265 did not. The mean score of the students who took
the test was 1028 (the national mean). Now imagine going to the
principal and asking how many of the 265 students who didn't
take the SAT could have scored 1180 or higher. The answer one
would expect to hear would be "none," and no more than one or
two, whereas the 4 percent assumption implies that about eleven
of the 265 students who did not take the SAT would have gotten
1180 or higher—an exceedingly implausible number. Using
4 percent as the upper bound gives us an estimate of 11.4 percent
of seventeen-year-olds who could have gotten 1180 or higher—
almost certainly an overestimate.

Method II. The second method takes advantage of the little-
known "national norm studies" that the College Board sponsored
periodically through 1983, based on nationally representative
samples of all students still in school, not just those headed for college. During the same years that the SAT scores of college-bound
seniors dropped precipitously, then began to rebound, the norm
studies showed remarkably level scores for the national population
(Herrnstein and Murray, 1994): 422. I use data from the 1983 norm
study. It does not report combined scores, so I used the separate
SAT-Verbal and SAT-Math benchmarks in Kobrin (2007), 590
and 610 respectively. Those are recentered scores that I converted
to pre-recentered scores using the College Board's conversion
tables, available at http://professionals.collegeboard.com/data-
reports-research/sat/equivalence-tables. After taking high-school

dropouts into account, the percentages in the 1983 norm study who reached the benchmarks were 9.2 and 9.9 percent for the SAT-Verbal and between 5.6 and 6.3 percent for the math. Since 1983, NAEP tells us that reading scores among seventeen-year-olds have been effectively flat. There is no reason to think that the 2005 figures would have been higher for today's youths. But NAEP does indicate an increase in math scores among seventeen-year-olds from 1983 to 2004. If we assume that the SAT scores from the 1983 norm study should be inflated commensurately, then the percentage of 2005 youth meeting the SAT-Math benchmark would have been about 7.5 to 8.2 percent.

Method III. The third method calls on the work of Meredith Frey and Douglas Detterman, who used the NLSY-79 to determine the IQ scores implied by SAT scores as of 1980. To get a score of 1100 on the pre-recentered test—the equivalent of an 1180 on the recentered test—implied an IQ of about 121.7 (Frey and Detterman [2004], and Douglas Detterman, personal communication). An IQ of 121.7 or higher includes the top 7.4 percent of the distribution. Since math scores went up between 1980 and 2005, let us assume that a parallel analysis done for 2005 would have shown a lower IQ equivalent. Using NAEP trends from 1980 to 2004 to make that adjustment, the IQ corresponding to the benchmark of 1100 (pre-recentered) would be approximately 119.5, cutting off the top 9.7 percent of the distribution.

Summarizing the lower-bound and upper-bound estimates of students who meet the College Board Benchmark as of 2005: Method I. 8.8 to 11.4 percent meeting the benchmark for the combined scores.

Method II. 9.2 to 9.9 percent meeting the benchmark on the

SAT-Verbal; 7.5 to 8.2 percent meeting the benchmark for the SAT-Math.

Method III. 7.4 to 9.7 percent meeting the benchmark for the combined scores.

If I had used a more plausible upper bound for the number of students who would have gotten 1180 or higher in calculating the results for method I, the three sets of results would have been close to identical. There is reason for confidence that the range given in the text—9 to 12 percent—encloses the true number, with the most realistic best guess being that the true number is about 10 percent.

73 On the length of sentences, the well-regarded high-school history textbook is John A. Garraty's *The Story of America: Beginnings to 1914* (New York: Holt, Rinehart and Winston, 1991).

74 The rankings of the vocabulary items come from the British National Corpus (BNC), described as "a 100 million word collection of samples of written and spoken language from a wide range of sources, designed to represent an accurate cross-section of current English usage." The 86,800 items include all the words that occur at least twice in the BNC. You may find the ranking for any word at www.wordcount.org. Since the BNC is based on British sources, I checked for words that would have a much different ranking in American English than in British English. There were none in the chosen passages.

75 On the calculation of the "too many" ratio, it is important to take into account the number of high-school dropouts, which can be estimated from the percentage of high-school freshmen who graduate from high school, and the number of first-time college freshmen who did not go to college directly from high school. For the

latter number, I assumed that all first-time freshmen ages eighteen and younger had gone directly from high school to college, and that 50 percent of all those who entered at age nineteen had gone directly from high school to college. Since first-time freshmen who are nineteen constitute only 29 percent of incoming freshmen, the choice of any reasonable estimate of the proportion of nineteen-year-olds who went directly to college has little effect on the "too many ratio." Sources for the data were the *Digest of Education Statistics 2006*, Tables 99 and 184, and unpublished data from the 2003–2004 Beginning Postsecondary Students Longitudinal Study provided by the National Center for Education Statistics. Applying these figures, it can be estimated that, as of 2005, about 4,100,000 American young people would have been eligible for enrollment as freshmen if everyone completed high school.

In the first iteration for calculating the "too many" ratio, I used the high end of the range of people who can absorb college-level material, 20 percent. Based on the NLSY-79, it may be assumed that about 80 percent of all those in the top 20 percent of academic ability enroll in four-year colleges directly out of high school. In that case, the expected number of incoming freshmen in 2005 should have been about 656,000. The actual number of first-time freshmen who had come directly from high school was approximately 1.2 million—about 1.8 times the "should" number. When I use the 15 percent cutoff instead, it should be assumed that about 85 percent of the eligible population enrolls as freshmen (the higher the IQ, the higher the probability that an American child goes to college). In that case, we should expect about 523,000 freshmen instead of 1.2 million, and the actual-to-should ratio is 2.3. When I use the 10 percent cutoff, it should be assumed that about 90 percent of all of the intellectually eligible enroll. In that case, we should have 369,000 freshmen instead of 1.2 million, and the "too many" ratio becomes 3.3. For the relationship of IQ to probability of college attendance, see Herrnstein and Murray (1994): 33–37.

75 The quotation from Mill is taken from Mill (1867): 217, available online at Google Books.

76–8 In the twenty years since *Cultural Literacy* was written, Hirsch has written several follow-up books. The most recent is Hirsch (2006). On the relationship of core knowledge to reading comprehension, Hirsch calls upon the distinction between reading as a process of decoding strings of letters and as the extraction of meaning from strings of words. At the beginning, learning to read is indeed a matter of learning to decode strings of letters and associate them with known words. Children at a wide range of linguistic ability can become competent at decoding. But as soon as this simplest level is left behind, background information begins to become important. Almost any text, whether in a newspaper or a novel or a third-grade reader, assumes that you have information at your disposal that the text itself need not explain. Two examples drawn from Hirsch (1987) illustrate how decisively background information affects our understanding of even the simplest text:

> *The punter kicked the ball.*
> *The golfer kicked the ball.*

These two five-word sentences, differing in just one word, call up completely different mental images of what the ball looks like, how and why the ball was kicked, and even the kicker's state of mind—but only if the reader knows something about football and golf. Just knowing the dictionary definitions of "punter," "golfer," "kick," and "ball" is not enough.

Now consider a sentence that uses the phrase *Achilles' heel*. If you do not know at least a little about Greek myths you cannot understand what you are reading. If a sentence uses the phrase "classical music" and you do not know at least a little about classical music and how it relates to other kinds of music, you cannot understand what you are reading. Reading speed is involved as well as reading comprehension. In all of these examples, your reading speed will slow to a crawl as you try to infer what the sentences mean from incomplete information. These examples are backed by an extensive research literature on the importance of background information to reading speed and comprehension that Hirsch reviews.

77–81 Regarding the Core Knowledge curriculum, you may examine an outline at www.coreknowledge.org. For a full description of the third-grade curriculum, including specific texts used to teach it, see Holdren and Hirsch (1996). On the quality of the Frederick County school system: According to a respected national survey (the 2007 edition of *Quality Counts*, conducted by the organization that publishes *Education Week*, and shown at http://www.edweek.org/ew/articles/2008/01/10/18sos.h27.html), Maryland's statewide system ranks third in the nation. The test scores from Frederick County's public schools are above the Maryland average (Maryland State Assessment data for 2007 taken from http://www.baltimoresun.com/news/education/bal-msareports2007,0,2020297.htmlstory).

My wife and I left our children in the Frederick County public schools because in many ways they were just fine. The facilities were good and the school environments were nurturing, orderly, and safe. Most of the principals and teachers were competent and dedicated, only a few were conspicuously poor, and several were excellent. Three were the finest K–12 teachers, public or private, that my wife and I have ever known. They deserve to be named: Frank Booth, Steve Nikirk, and Lee Vogtman.

I did not use cosmetic shortcomings in the Frederick County website to make its curriculum look bad. On the contrary, my wife and I knew that mathematics and writing were taught more rigorously in the classroom than the website description would lead one to believe, so I omitted the website's descriptions of those subjects from the table. By the same token, we also knew that the website's characterization of Frederick County's third-grade curriculum for everything else accurately reflected what was taught in the classroom and assigned as homework. You may check the website for your local school system and compare it with the Core Knowledge curriculum for yourself.

81 *On Liberty* was accessed through Google Books.

82 Rawls's formulation is in Rawls (1971): 426. Aristotle's discussion is mostly in books seven and ten of *Nichomachean Ethics*.

86 The examples of courses that fulfill the distribution requirements and the data on distribution requirements in the fifty colleges are taken from Latzer (2004): 3–4, 26. On the topics for course requirements, the obvious omission is a course in Western Civilization. The problems of deciding what courses qualified proved to be so difficult that the category had to be dropped. For another excellent discussion of the deficiencies in distribution requirements, see Mathews (2005).

91–2 On the reasons that people with BAs make more than people without BAs, an extensive technical literature tries to get into the black box linking education with earnings. Human capital theory (Becker, 1962 and Schultz, 1962) says that education adds skills, and greater skills lead to higher earnings. Screening and signaling theories (Arrow, 1973 and Spence, 1973) say that employers use educational credentials as a screen for qualities they want (ability, perseverance, etc.) and students use those credentials to signal that they possess such qualities. I assume that the human capital theory in higher education applies most strongly to occupations requiring specific knowledge and skills taught in the classroom (e.g., engineering, medicine, and law), and is least relevant to occupations for which the specific knowledge and skills can be taught on the job (e.g., journalism, many entry-level business jobs). My point in the text is not that the BA for history majors and English lit majors is completely worthless in a human capital sense (it usually has some value, I am willing to assume), but that employers care mostly about its screening value.

93 The occupational income data are available at http://www.bls .gov/oes/oes_dl.htm.

98 On the time that students spend studying, three surveys sponsored by the Pew Charitable Trusts are conducted annually: the National Survey of Student Engagement (NSSE), the Faculty Survey of Student Engagement (FSSE), and the Beginning College Survey of Student Engagement, focusing on entering classes (BSSE). The figures in the text are taken from their 2007 annual reports, available at http://nsse.iub.edu/index.cfm. The first administration of the BSSE occurred in the summer of 2007.

98 The quotation from the Duke administrator comes from Seaman (2005): 66.

99 The survey of student priorities is reported in Sacks (1996): 55.

99 The quotation about students who argued about the right answer comes from Twenge (2006): 28.

100 The Berkeley professor is quoted in Seaman (2005): 62.

100 On the excesses of campus life, Seaman (2005) has the most complete presentation. Other useful discussions are found in Sacks (1996), Schneider and Stevenson (1999), and Twenge (2006). Tom Wolfe's fictional account of contemporary college life, *I Am Charlotte Simmons* (Wolfe, 2005), reflects extensive journalistic research.

101 On the seriousness of students who come to college after several years away, I am reporting anecdotal evidence from college professors with whom I have discussed this issue. The quotation about students as consumers comes from Sacks (1996): 162.

103 The figure regarding guidance counselors comes from Schneider and Stevenson (1999): 1292.

104 The figures on students aspiring to professional jobs and with misaligned ambitions come from Schneider and Stevenson (1999): 5, 81. The book has an extended discussion of misaligned ambitions and associated topics.

104 The data on students completing their college degree within five years come from *Digest of Education Statistics 2006*, Table 317.

Chapter 4

107–8 William F. Buckley's famous dictum dates from an essay he wrote in 1956, which he quotes approvingly in a later book (Buckley, 1963): 103.

109–10 Steven Goldberg's analogy between IQ and weight in NFL tackles comes from Goldberg (2003): 51–52.

110 On the relationship of IQ to occupation, see Gottfredson (1997), available at http://www.udel.edu/educ/gottfredson/reprints/1997whygmatters.pdf, and Herrnstein and Murray (1994): chapters 2 and 3.

110 Population figures are taken from the *Statistical Abstract of the United States* for 2007, Table 11, available online at http://www.census.gov/. The resident population ages twenty-five to sixty-four as of 2005 was 156,845,000, which I extrapolated to 160 million as of 2008.

111 The *U.S. News & World Report* rankings can be found at http://colleges.usnews.rankingsandreviews.com/usnews/edu/college/rankings/brief/t1natudoc_brief.php.

111 The data regarding college attendance by academic ability were taken from the 1979 cohort of the NLSY and reported in Herrnstein and Murray (1994): 33–37. On the distribution of the gifted across campuses, a great deal depends on the definition of *gifted*. The most prestigious schools get an extraordinary proportion of those in the very top percentiles of academic ability. When Richard Herrnstein and I looked at the issue in the early 1990s, just ten schools—Harvard, Yale, Stanford, University of Pennsylvania, Princeton, Brown, University of California–Berkeley, Cornell, Dartmouth, and Columbia—got 31 percent of students who scored 700+ on the (pre-recentered) SAT-Verbal. Harvard and Yale alone accounted for 10 percent of them (Herrnstein and Murray, 1994): 43.

112 The estimates of the education of the gifted are based on the author's analysis of the NLSY-79.

113–16 For a complementary discussion of college-level training in verbal expression, see Bok (2006), chapter 4.

114 Data on the number of students scoring 700 or higher are taken from the annual reports of the College Board. See Herrnstein and Murray (1994): 775, note 32 for a discussion of the estimate for 1967. Regarding the assumption that almost all seventeen-year-olds who could get a 700+ score were taking the SAT as of 1967, I should note that if the assumption is wrong, and that instead that proportion has increased over time (the proportion cannot have decreased, given the overall increase in the proportion of college-bound students taking the SAT), the analysis presented in the text *understates* the magnitude of the drop in the percentage of seventeen-year-olds who got a 700+ score. For an analysis of the SAT score decline, see Murray and Herrnstein (1992).

Regarding the recentered SAT: In 1995, the SAT reset the means for both the SAT-Verbal and the SAT-Math to 500. These represented the means when the SAT was normed in 1940. The effect of the recentering was to raise scores—the pre-recentered means in 1994 were 423 for the SAT-Verbal and 479 for the SAT-Math. Details on recentering may be obtained at http://professionals.collegeboard.com/research/pdf/200211_20702.pdf.

117–18 For a complementary discussion of college-level training in quantitative reasoning, see Bok (2006), chapter 5.

120 On the evolution of American higher education, an excellent history is Thelin (2004). Kronman (2007) focuses specifically on the evolution of the curriculum with regard to a liberal education. The Kronman quotation comes from page 239.

122–23 On the two great ethical systems, the original sources are Aristotle's *Nichomachean Ethics* and Confucius's *The Analects*, both available through Google Books.

124 On the moral content of the McGuffey Readers, look up some of them at Google Books. The contrast with the moral content of today's curriculum is striking.

128–29 On the trigger for the self-esteem movement, see Branden (1969). The quotation from the California Task Force is taken from Mecca, Smelser, and Vasconcellos (1989). On the recent debunking of self-esteem, Baumeister, Campbell, Kreuger, and Vohs (2005) is the key source. A *Scientific American* account written for a general audience is available online at http://www .sciam.com/article.cfm?chanID=sa006&colID=1&articleID= 000CB565-F330-11BE-AD0683414B7F0000. See also Twenge (2006), chapter 2.

130 On the perverse effects of praise, Bronson (2007) pulls together the several strands of scholarly research. The meta-analysis mentioned in the text is Henderlong and Lepper (2002).

132 On George Christian's maxim, I heard him say it, or read of him saying it, shortly after he left his job as press secretary in 1969, and it impressed me so powerfully that I never forgot it. But I have not been able to find a source for it.

Chapter 5

133 Some personal disclosure is appropriate as I begin to lay out my recommendations—people who talk about what's best for other people's children have been known to make different decisions for their own lives and their own children (viz., politicians who sing the praises of the public schools while sending their own children to private schools). I attended public schools in a small Midwestern town and then went to private universities for both undergraduate and graduate studies. My wife attended the same public schools,

two state universities, got her PhD at a private university, and was on the faculty of a state university. My two elder children went to a suburban public school system for several years and then transferred to a private school. My two younger children attended public schools in a predominantly blue-collar and farming area. The youngest was home-schooled during the eighth grade. All four attended or attend private colleges.

136 On the relationship of academic ability and academic achievement, it is important to distinguish between the variation in scores that will be found to exist and the variation that the schools can do anything about. Let's stay with the example of students tested in first grade for linguistic ability and tested in eighth grade for reading achievement. The correlation between the two sets of scores will be high, but even a correlation of +.6 or +.7 leaves a great deal of variation in scores. That variation is caused by a host of things, ranging from measurement error in the tests themselves to the home environment (does Mom check the homework every night?) to personal qualities of the individual student such as self-discipline. So students with the same first-grade score on a test of linguistic ability will vary widely on their reading ability in eighth grade, despite the high correlation between ability and achievement. The first issue is whether the school that the child attended is an important cause of the variation. If it is not (as the Coleman Report first found), then there are no off-the-shelf ways to make some schools do much better in raising reading performance. The second issue is whether some of the important causes of the variation are causes that a school can affect. For example, Duckworth and Seligman (2005) report evidence that self-discipline can be

more important than IQ in predicting certain kinds of academic outcomes among eighth-graders. Is it possible for schools to have an important effect on self-discipline? Answering that question requires other kinds of research and can involve experimental methods for encouraging self-discipline. If it is found that the schools can improve self-discipline, then schools have a potential strategy for improving achievement independently of academic ability. That's why continued research into the ways that children learn and the ways that their personalities develop can ultimately improve education. The summary statement about the current state of knowledge: Variation in student outcomes within a given ability level exists; the degree to which we know how to manipulate the causes of that variation is small; and the degree to which the school is a source of that variation is small.

137 On the assets of foundations, the numbers were obtained from http://foundationcenter.org/findfunders/topfunders/top 100assets.html and http://www.gatesfoundation.org/Media Center/FactSheet/.

140–41 On the first-grade assessment of children, I omit bodily-kinesthetic and musical abilities. Elementary education can proceed in all its essentials without testing for a child's bodily-kinesthetic and musical ability, whereas it is affected directly by extremes, high or low, in the five abilities that are part of the battery. And, as a practical matter, most schools efficiently identify athletic and musical talent anyway.

141 On expenditures per pupil, see *Digest of Educational Statistics 2006*, Table 167. In some of the worst big-city school systems in the United States, it is much higher yet (the Washington, DC,

public schools now spend about $15,000 per student, extrapolating from 2003–2004 expenditures as shown in Table 170 in the same source).

144 Regarding the phrase *transforming experience*, I am drawing specifically from the discussion in Walters and Gardner (1986). For a wide-ranging set of articles that survey the state of knowledge about education of the gifted, see Benbow and Lubinski (1996).

147–50 On the forgotten half, the indispensable source is Rosenbaum (2001). On the perceived lack of incentives for high school students to work, see chapter 3. This lack of incentives extends to college-bound students who are not interested in a selective school. Rosenbaum also presents a full discussion with references to the literature on the real absence of short-term payoffs for getting good grades (chapter 5). There may be long-term payoffs (causation is unclear), but not surprisingly, adolescents do not recognize these. For a review of the technical literature on the role of high-school counselors and an excellent original study, see chapter 4 of Rosenbaum (2001). For a useful narrative account of counseling in three different types of high school, see chapter 8 of Csikszentmihalyi and Schneider (2000). For a review of the empirical findings about vocational-education graduates compared to those of comparable academic ability who remain in an academic track, see Bishop and Mane (2004).

151–53 The number of students in private schools comes from *Digest of Education Statistics 2006*, Table 55. The data on charter schools come from *The Condition of Education*, http://nces .ed.gov/programs/coe/2007/section4/indicator32.asp. To find a charter school near you, try http://www.edreform.com/ index.cfm?fuseAction=section&pSectionID=5&CFID=9003774

&CFTOKEN=21572744. On the number of home-schooled children, see http://nces.ed.gov/pubs2006/homeschool/index.asp. The National Home Education Research Institute estimates that the number of children being home-schooled had risen to more than 2 million by 2007 and is as high as 2.4 million, but that estimate is unverified. See http://www.nheri.org/. For a recent list of voucher and tax-credit programs, see Enlow (2008), downloadable at http://www.friedmanfoundation.org/friedman/downloadFile.do?id=268.

156 The information about the CPA examination is taken from http://www.cpa-exam.org.

157 On degrees awarded by major, see *Digest of Educational Statistics 2006,* Table 254.

159 On the existing certification industry, visit http://www.prometric.com/default.htm or http://www.vue.com/ to get a sense of the range of testing that already exists.

161 On the spillover effect of discovering that one enjoys learning, my views parallel many of Howard Gardner's arguments for a curriculum that teaches a few topics in great depth (Gardner, 1999): chapters 7 to 9. We differ in that Gardner wants this approach applied to K–12, whereas I think those are the years (especially K–8) when a broad foundation of factual knowledge must be acquired.

163 For the compelling evidence that attending elite schools isn't nearly as valuable as parents think, see Dale and Kreuger (2002). Regarding the two kinds of foolishness that parents exhibit when paying for their children's college education, I plead innocent to the first type, guilty to the second type.

Bibliography

Ackerman, P. L., & Heggestad, E. D. (1997). Intelligence, personality, and interests: Evidence for overlapping traits. *Psychological Bulletin, 121*(2), 219–245.

Anyon, J. (1997). *Ghetto Schooling: A Political Economy of Urban Educational Reform.* New York: Teachers College Press.

Arrow, K. (1973). Higher education as a filter. *Journal of Public Economics, 2,* 193–216.

Barnard, J., Frangakis, C. E., Hill, J. L., & Rubin, D. B. (2003). Principal Stratification Approach to Broken Randomized Experiments: A Case Study of School Choice Vouchers in New York City. *Journal of the American Statistical Association, 98*(462), 299–311.

Baumeister, A. A., & Bacharach, V. R. (2000). Early generic educational intervention has no enduring effect on intelligence and does not prevent mental retardation: The Infant Health and Development Program. *Intelligence, 28*(3), 161–192.

Baumeister, R. F., Campbell, J. D., Kreuger, J. I., & Vohs, K. D. (2005). Exploding the Self Esteem Myth. *Scientific American, 292,* 84–91.

Becker, G. S. (1962). Investment in human capital: A theoretical approach. *Journal of Political Economy, 70*(5 [part 2]), 9–49.

Benbow, C. P., & Lubinski, D. (eds.). (1996). *Intellectual Talent: Psychometric and Social Issues.* Baltimore: The Johns Hopkins University Press.

Bishop, J., & Mane, F. (2004). The impacts of career-technical education on high school labor market success. *Economics of Education Review*, *23*(4), 381–402.

Blair, C., & Wahlsten, D. (2002). Why early intervention works: A reply to Baumeister and Bacharach. *Intelligence*, *30*(2), 129–140.

Bok, D. (2006). *Our Underachieving Colleges: A Candid Look at How Much Students Learn and Why They Should Be Learning More*. Princeton, NJ: Princeton University Press.

Branden, N. (1969). *The Psychology of Self-Esteem: A New Concept of Man's Psychological Nature*. Los Angeles: Nash Publishing.

Bronson, P. (2007, February 11). How not to talk to your kids: The inverse power of praise. *New York*, 24–29.

Brooks-Gunn, J., et al. (1994). Early intervention in low-birth-weight premature infants. *JAMA*, *272*(16), 1257–1262.

Brooks-Gunn, J., Liaw, F., & Klebanov, P. K. (1992). Effects of early intervention on cognitive function of low birth weight preterm infants. *Journal of Pediatrics*, *120*(3), 350–359.

Buckley, W. F., Jr. (1963) *Rumbles Left and Right*. New York: G. P. Putnam's Sons.

Campbell, F. A., Pungello, E. P., Miller-Johnson, S., Burchinal, M., & Ramey, C. T. (2001). The development of cognitive and academic abilities: Growth curves from an early childhood educational experiment. *Developmental Psychology*, *37*(2), 231–242.

Carroll, J. B. (1995). Reflections on Stephen Jay Gould's *The Mismeasure of Man* (1981): A retrospective review. *Intelligence*, *21*, 121–134.

Coleman, J. S., et al. (1966). *Equality of Educational Opportunity*. Washington, DC: U.S. Office of Education.

Coleman, J. S., Hoffer, T., & Kilgore, S. (1982). *High School Achievement: Public, Catholic, and Private Schools*. New York: Basic Books.

Colom, R., Jung, R. E., & Haier, R. J. (2006). Distributed brain sites for the *g*-factor of intelligence. *NeuroImage, 31*, 1359–1365.

Cowen, J. M. (2007). School choice as a latent variable: Estimating the "complier average causal effect" of vouchers in Charlotte. *Policy Studies Journal,* forthcoming.

Csikszentmihalyi, M., & Schneider, B. (2000). *Becoming Adult: How Teenagers Prepare for the World of Work.* New York: Basic Books.

Dale, S. B., & Kreuger, A. B. (2002). Estimating the payoff to attending a more selective college: An application of selection on observables and unobservables. *Quarterly Journal of Economics, 117*(4), 1491–1527.

Deary, I. J., Strand, S., Smith, P., & Fernandes, C. (2007). Intelligence and educational achievement. *Intelligence, 35*(1), 23–40.

Doidge, N. (2007). *The Brain That Changes Itself: Stories of Personal Triumph from the Frontiers of Brain Science.* New York: Viking.

Duckworth, A. L., & Seligman, M. E. P. (2005). Self-discipline outdoes IQ in predicting academic performance of adolescents. *Psychological Science, 16*(12), 939–944.

Enlow, R. C. (2008). *Grading School Choice: Evaluating School Choice Programs by the Friedman Gold Standard:* The Friedman Foundation for Educational Choice.

Frey, M. C., & Detterman, D. K. (2004). Scholastic assessment or *g*: The relationship between the Scholastic Assessment Test and general cognitive ability. *Psychological Science, 15*(6), 373–378.

Gardner, H. (1983). *Frames of Mind: The Theory of Multiple Intelligences* (1985 ed.). New York: Basic Books.

Gardner, H. (1999). *The Disciplined Mind: Beyond Facts and Standardized Tests, the K–12 Education That Every Child Deserves.* New York: Simon & Schuster.

Geher, G. (ed.). (2004). *Measuring Emotional Intelligence: Common Ground and Controversy.* Hauppauge, NY: Nova Science Publishers.

Goldberg, S. (2003). *Fads and Fallacies in the Social Sciences.* Amherst, NY: Humanity Books.

Goleman, D. (1995). *Emotional Intelligence: Why It Can Matter More Than IQ.* New York: Bantam.

Good, J. M. M., Aggleton, J. P., Kentridge, R. W., Barker, J. G. M., & Neave, N. J. (1997). Measuring musical aptitude in children: On the role of age, handedness, scholastic achievement, and socioeconomic status. *Psychology of Music, 25,* 57–69.

Gottfredson, L. S. (1997). Why *g* matters: the complexity of everyday life. *Intelligence, 24*(1), 79–132.

Gould, S. J. (1981). *The Mismeasure of Man.* New York: W. W. Norton.

Greene, J. P. (2001). Vouchers in Charlotte. *Education Matters, 1*(2), 55–60.

Greene, J. P., Peterson, P. E., & Du, J. (1999). School choice in Milwaukee: A randomized experiment. In P. E. Peterson & B. C. Hassell (eds.), *Learning from School Choice* (pp. 335–56). Washington, DC: Brookings Institution.

Haier, R. J., Jung, R. E., Yeo, R. A., Head, K., & Alkire, M. T. (2004). Structural brain variation and general intelligence. *NeuroImage, 23*(1), 425–433.

Heckman, J., & Masterov, D. V. (2007). *The Productivity Argument for Investing in Young Children.* Bonn, DE: IZA.

Henderlong, J., & Lepper, M. R. (2002). The effects of praise on children's intrinsic motivation: A review and synthesis. *Psychological Bulletin, 128*(5), 774–795.

Herman, J. L., & Haertel, E. H. (eds.). (2005). *Uses and Misuses of Data for Educational Accountability and Improvement.* Malden, MA: Wiley-Blackwell.

Herrnstein, R. J., & Murray, C. (1994). *The Bell Curve: Intelligence and Class Structure in American Life.* New York: Free Press.

Hirsch, E. D., Jr. (1987). *Cultural Literacy: What Every American Needs to Know.* Boston: Houghton Mifflin.

Hirsch, E. D., Jr. (2006). *The Knowledge Deficit: Closing the Shocking Education Gap for American Children.* Boston: Houghton Mifflin.

Holdren, J., & Hirsch, E. D., Jr. (eds.). (1996). *Books to Build On: A Grade-by-Grade Resource Guide for Parents and Teachers.* New York: Delta.

Howell, W. G., & Peterson, P. E. (2006). *The Education Gap: Vouchers and Urban Schools* (Revised ed.). Washington, DC: Brookings Institution Press.

Irvine, U. O. C. (2004, Oct. 21). Early Life Stress Can Inhibit Development of Brain-Cell Communication Zones. *ScienceDaily.*

Jensen, A. R. (1998). *The g Factor: The Science of Mental Ability.* Westport, CT: Praeger.

Judge, T. A., Bono, J. E., Ilies, R., & Gerhardt, M. W. (2002). Personality and leadership: A qualitative and quantitative review. *Journal of Applied Psychology, 87,* 765–780.

Judge, T. A., Colbert, A. E., & Ilies, R. (2004). Intelligence and leadership: A quantitative review and test of theoretical propositions. *Journal of Applied Psychology, 89*(3), 542–552.

Kobrin, J. L. (2007). *Determining SAT Benchmarks for College Readiness.* New York: College Board.

Koretz, D. (2007). The pending reauthorization of NCLB: An opportunity to rethink the basic strategy. In G. L. Sunderman (ed.), *Holding NCLB Accountable: Achieving Accountability, Equity, and School Reform.* Thousand Oaks, CA: Corwin Press.

Kosters, M. H., & Mast, B. D. (2003). *Closing the Education Achievement Gap: Is Title I Working?* Washington, DC: AEI Press.

Kozol, J. (1967). *Death at an Early Age: The Destruction of the Hearts and Minds of Negro Children.* New York: Houghton Mifflin.

Kreuger, A. B., & Zhu, P. (2003). Comment on "Principal Stratification Approach to Broken Randomized Experiments: A Case Study of School Choice Vouchers in New York City." *Journal of the American Statistical Association, 98*(462), 314–318.

Kronman, A. T. (2007). *Education's End: Why Our Colleges and Universities Have Given Up on the Meaning of Life.* New Haven: Yale University Press.

Latzer, B. (2004). *The Hollow Core: Failure of the General Education Curriculum:* American Council of Trustees and Alumni.

Lazar, I., & Darlington, R. (1982). Lasting effects of early education: A report from the consortium for longitudinal studies. *Monographs of the Society for Research in Child Development, 47*(2–3, Serial No. 195).

Lee, J. (2006). *Tracking Achievement Gaps and Assessing the Impact of NCLB on the Gaps: An In-Depth Look into National and State Reading and Math Outcome Trends.* Cambridge MA: The Civil Rights Project, Harvard University.

Locurto, C. (1990). The malleability of IQ as judged from adoption studies. *Intelligence, 14,* 275–292.

Loveless, T. (2004). *The 2004 Brown Center Report on American Education.* Washington, DC: Brookings Institution.

Loveless, T. (2007). *The 2007 Brown Center Report on American Education.* Washington, DC: Brookings Institution.

Lynn, R., & Gault, A. (1986). The relation of music ability to general intelligence and the major primaries. *Research in Education, 36,* 59–64.

Matarazzo, J. D. (1972). *Wechsler's Measurement and Appraisal of Adult Intelligence.* New York: Oxford University Press.

Mathews, J. (2005). Caveat lector: Unexamined assumptions about quality in higher education. In R. H. Hersh & J. Merrow (eds.), *Declining by Degrees: Higher Education at Risk* (pp. 47–59). New York: Palgrave Macmillan.

Matthews, G., Zeidner, M., & Roberts, R. (2004). *Emotional Intelligence: Science and Myth.* Cambridge, MA: MIT Press.

Mayer, J. D., Salovey, P., & Caruso, D. R. (2004). Emotional intelligence: Theory, findings, and implications. *Psychological Inquiry, 15,* 197–215.

McCormick, M. C., Brooks-Gunn, J., Buka, S. L., et al. (2006). Early intervention in low birth weight premature infants: Results at 18 years of age for the Infant Health and Development Program. *Pediatrics, 117,* 771–780.

McCormick, M. C., McCarton, C., Tonascia, J., & Brooks-Gunn, J. (1993). Early educational intervention for very low birth weight infants: Results from the Infant Health and Development Program. *Journal of Pediatrics, 123*(4), 527–533.

McLoyd, V. C. (1998). Socioeconomic disadvantage and child development. *American Psychologist, 53*(2), 185–204.

Mecca, A., Smelser, N. J., & Vasconcellos, J. (eds.). (1989). *The Social Importance of Self-Esteem.* Berkeley, CA: University of California Press.

Mill, J. S. (1867). Inaugural Address Delivered to the University of St. Andrews. In *Essays on Equality, Law, and Education* (pp. 217–257). London: Longmans, Green, Reader, and Dyer.

Mosteller, F., & Moynihan, D. P. (eds.). (1972). *On Equality of Educational Opportunity.* New York: Random House.

Murray, C. (1984). *Losing Ground: American Social Policy 1950–1980.* New York: Basic Books.

Murray, C. (1988). *In Pursuit: Of Happiness and Good Government.* New York: Simon & Schuster.

Murray, C. (1997). *What It Means to Be a Libertarian: A Personal Interpretation.* New York: Broadway Books.

Murray, C., & Herrnstein, R. J. (1992). What's really behind the SAT-score decline. *The Public Interest,* no. *106,* 32–56.

Noguera, P. A. (2003). *City Schools and the American Dream: Reclaiming the Promise of Public Education.* New York: Teachers College Press.

Park, G., Lubinski, D., & Benbow, C. P. (2007). Contrasting intellectual patterns predict creativity in the arts and sciences: Tracking intellectually precocious youth over 25 years. *Psychological Science, 18* (11), 948–952.

Parker, L. O. N. (2007a, Nov. 12, 2007). For Jonathan Lewis, It's Fourth and Goal. *Washington Post,* p. A1+.

Parker, L. O. N. (2007b, Dec. 23, 2007). Lessons in reality. *Washington Post,* p. A01+.

Parker, L. O. N. (2007c, Nov. 10, 2007). Will Jonathan graduate? *Washington Post,* p. A01+.

Rawls, J. (1971). *A Theory of Justice.* Cambridge, Mass.: Harvard University Press.

Reeve, C. L., Meyer, R. D., & Bonaccio, S. (2006). Intelligence-personality associations reconsidered: The importance of distinguishing between general and narrow dimensions of intelligence. *Intelligence, 34,* 387–402.

Rosenbaum, J. (2001). *Beyond College for All: Career Paths for the Forgotten Half.* New York: Russell Sage Foundation.

Rouse, C. E. (1998). Private school vouchers and student achievement: An evaluation of the Milwaukee Parental Choice Program. *Quarterly Journal of Economics, 113*(2), 553–602.

Sacks, P. (1996). *Generation X Goes to College: An Eye-Opening Account of Teaching in Postmodern America*. Chicago: Open Court Publishing.

Schneider, B., & Stevenson, D. (1999). *The Ambitious Generation: America's Teenagers, Motivated but Directionless*. New Haven: Yale University Press.

Schultz, T. W. (1962). Investment in human beings. *Journal of Political Economy, 70*(5 [part 2]).

Seaman, B. (2005). *Binge: What Your College Student Won't Tell You*. New York: John Wiley & Sons.

Shuter, R. (1968). *The Psychology of Musical Talent*. New York: Silver Burdett.

Spearman, C. S. (1904). "General intelligence," objectively determined and measured. *American Journal of Psychology, 15*, 201–209.

Spence, M. (1973). Job market signalling. *Quarterly Journal of Economics, 87*, 355–374.

Spitz, H. H. (1986). *The Raising of Intelligence: A Selected History of Attempts to Raise Retarded Intelligence*. Hillsdale, NJ: Lawrence Erlbaum Associates.

Spitz, H. H. (1992). Does the Carolina Abecedarian early intervention project prevent sociocultural mental retardation? *Intelligence, 16*, 225–237.

Spitz, H. H. (2001). Attempts to raise intelligence. In M. Anderson (ed.), *The Development of Intelligence*. Hove, UK: Psychology Press.

Stedman, L. C., & Kaestle, C. F. (1991). Literacy and reading performance in the United States from 1880 to the present. In C. F. Kaestle, H. Damon-Moore, L. C. Stedman, K. Tinsley, & W. V. Trollinger (eds.), *Literacy in the United States: Readers and Reading Since 1880* (pp. 75–128). New Haven: Yale University Press.

Stern, S. (2003). *Breaking Free: Public School Lessons and the Imperative of School Choice*. San Francisco: Encounter Books.

Sternberg, R. J. (1995). For whom *The Bell Curve* tolls. *Psychological Science*, 257–262.

Thelin, J. R. (2004). *A History of American Higher Education*. Baltimore: The Johns Hopkins University Press.

Thompson, P., Cannon, T. D., Narr, K. L., Erp, T., Poutanen, V., Huttunen, M., et al. (2001). Genetic influences on brain structure. *Nature Neuroscience, 4*(12), 1–6.

Twenge, J. M. (2006). *Generation Me: Why Today's Young Americans Are More Confident, Assertive, Entitled—and More Miserable Than Ever Before*. New York: Free Press.

Walberg, H. J. (2007). *School Choice: The Findings*. Washington, DC: Cato Institute.

Walters, J., & Gardner, H. (1986). The crystallizing experience: Discovering an intellectual gift. In R. J. Sternberg & J. E. Davidson (eds.), *Conceptions of Giftedness* (pp. 306–331). New York: Cambridge University Press.

Watkins, M. W., Lei, P.-W., & Canivez, G. L. (2007). Psychometric intelligence and achievement: A cross-lagged panel analysis. *Intelligence, 35*(1), 59–68.

Wolf, P., Gutmann, B., Puma, M., Rizzo, L., Eissa, N., & Silverberg, M. (2007). *Evaluation of the DC Opportunity Scholarship Program: Impacts After One Year*. Washington, DC: U.S. Department of Education, Institute of Education Sciences.

Wolfe, T. (2005). *I Am Charlotte Simmons: A Novel*. New York: Picador.

Index

About the Author

Charles Murray is the W. H. Brady Scholar at the American Enterprise Institute in Washington, D.C. He is the author of two of the most widely debated and influential social policy books of the last three decades, *Losing Ground: American Social Policy 1950–1980* and, with the late Richard J. Herrnstein, *The Bell Curve: Intelligence and Class Structure in American Life.* He lives with his family in Burkittsville, Maryland.